'Hope for Justice truly are modern-day a

'Incredibly brave and life-saving work.'

Bear Grylls, Chief Scout

'For many years, I have admired the passion, drive and excellence that Hope for Justice has applied in the fight against human trafficking. Ben Cooley is a visionary leader who has an incredible gift: he has not only started an organization, he has also built a movement. This book is an excellent resource for anyone wanting to learn about the highs and lows of leadership, and how to deliver their vision.'

Sir Brian Souter, founder and Chairman, Stagecoach Group

'The story of Hope for Justice is an important one. Throughout the UK and across the world, the issues of human trafficking and modern-day slavery have become increasingly high profile. The work that Hope for Justice does to combat these injustices is inspiring. This book not only shares the heart of the organization but also some great insights into how slavery can be eradicated for good. I would highly commend the charity and this book to anyone.'

Ram Gidoomal, Chairman, Traidcraft

'Ben Cooley is an inspiring leader. He has met every challenge with great wisdom and humility. Hope for Justice has become a key player in the fight against modern-day slavery; its members' influence and experience as practitioners and advocates are incredibly important for businesses, governments and individuals to learn from. I would highly commend this book and hope it can be a catalyst for genuine transformation.'

Sir Peter Vardy, Chairman, Vardy Group

'More than two years ago, with input from leading stakeholders and industry experts, we created a bold vision not only to fight the horrific practice of modern-day slavery but to end it, and, in December 2016, the End Modern Slavery Initiative Act was signed into law. Hope for Justice played a critical role in those efforts, and I appreciate the work this important organization continues to do to rescue and restore victims of modern slavery.'

Bob Corker, US Senator for Tennessee

'*Impossible Is a Dare* is a powerful reminder that, when it comes to standing up for the vulnerable – such as victims of modern slavery – there is no excuse for inaction. Ben Cooley's story is full of compassion, inspiration and, importantly, action . . . It speaks to us all about the value of taking personal responsibility for the welfare of others.'

David Burrowes, MP for Enfield, Southgate

'Ben's vision for Hope for Justice is inspirational and his sacrifice truly humbling. This book moves seamlessly between the story of Ben's faith in starting this amazing organization, his obedience to the call of God on his life, and the stories of those people Hope for Justice seeks to help. I would recommend this book to all who are looking to do the impossible with their lives, in whatever way God is calling, and to take up the dare as Ben did – the world needs you!'

Tim Hughes, Worship Central

'I have a huge amount of respect for Ben and Hope for Justice. Their commitment to rescuing and restoring those trapped in slavery is an inspiration. This book is not only a call to end trafficking but a challenge to each one of us to overcome seemingly impossible situations in our own lives. A fantastic read!'

Steve McClaren, former manager, England football team

'This book reveals in part the ongoing journey of Ben Cooley and Hope for Justice, a journey that is both intentional and highly inspirational. I wholeheartedly commend *Impossible Is a Dare* to those committed to taking action against modern-day slavery.'

Mick Layton, Deputy Director (retired), Serious Organised Crime Agency

'Hope for Justice does incredible work around the world, and we are delighted to commend the organization and Ben to all readers.'

John and Debby Wright, National Directors, Vineyard Churches, UK and Ireland

'This is a book of stories – compassionate stories – of lovely human beings. Some have struggled with exploitation and barbaric treatment that no human being should suffer; others have faced the challenge of responding sacrificially and consistently to the glaring injustices in our world. These are all stories that need to be told, and Ben Cooley does that so well, weaving them into his own personal narrative. I know the book will find a wide audience. I believe it will also draw many people to reflect on the part they can play in the work of bringing greater hope for justice.'

Elaine Storkey, philosopher, sociologist, theologian and author of Scars Across Humanity: Understanding and overcoming violence against women

'This is much more than a business book or inspiring story – this is a rallying call to all of us to step up and meet the challenges in front of us. No great achievement has ever been easy – all it takes to get started is a commitment to pursue your passion. Ben will inspire, challenge and encourage you to get started.'

Michael O'Neil, CEO, Stewardship

'When Ben Cooley first heard about the plight of those caught in modern-day slavery, he was young and naive enough to believe that someone with audacious courage could see slavery cease within a generation. The crisis affects millions, but the cause that Ben lives for is to set free every enslaved individual . . . Read this book, we dare you!'

Glyn and Sophia Barrett, !Audacious Church, Manchester

Ben Cooley is an outstanding leader, an innovator and a passionate and determined crusader. His book reveals every aspect of his tenacious character. You will be stirred in your spirit and moved to action not only by his personality, which comes through every page of the book, but also by the stories that he tells.

Ken Costa, author and Dean, Leadership College, London

IMPOSSIBLE
IS A DARE
BEN COOLEY

(SPCK)

First published in Great Britain in 2017

Society for Promoting Christian Knowledge
36 Causton Street
London SW1P 4ST
www.spck.org.uk

British Library Cataloguing-in-Publication Data
A catalogue record for this book is available from the British Library.

ISBN: 978–0–281–07884–4
eBook ISBN: 978–0–281–07885–1

Typeset in Great Britain by CRB Associates, Potterhanworth, Lincolnshire
Manufacture managed by Jellyfish
First printed in Great Britain by CPI
Subsequently digitally printed in Great Britain

eBook by CRB Associates, Potterhanworth, Lincolnshire

Produced on paper from sustainable forests

Contents

Acknowledgements

If you had told me years ago that one day I would write a book, I wouldn't have believed you. I could never have written a book. It was impossible. Well, it turns out that this belief was only half true. I could never write a book . . . *alone*. This book and, more importantly, the stories told within it, could not have happened without so many different people. If I were to thank everyone by name, well . . . we'd need another book! So to all those I don't have space to mention here, thank you so much!

To Deb, Isabel and Lilly, thank you for just being the best! Life with you is the greatest adventure. A huge thank you as well to the rest of my family: Mum, Dad — you guys are amazing.

Rob and Marion, this story couldn't be told without you! Thank you for contributing to this book — and, more importantly, for investing so much time, wisdom (and patience!) in me.

Tony and Viv, the support you have given our family literally blows my mind. Thank you so much.

Glyn and Sophia . . . thanks for your guidance, leadership and friendship!

To all the team at Hope for Justice, what can I say? This story would not be the same without you. The work all of you do — from the oldest to the newest member — is invaluable, and this journey would not be as passionate, purposeful or, let's face it – fun – without you. And to all who attended book club throughout the years . . . do you reckon this one would make the cut?!

Gareth, thank you for your tireless work on this project – your passion for it has been there from the start and has never wavered. Thank you so much for everything you have brought to it. To the team at SPCK, to Steve and Elizabeth (you stars!), thank you for your guidance through the weird and wonderful world of publishing – I know I've not been the easiest of authors (after all, I think 'impossible' is a dare!) but I have been truly humbled by the hard work and dedication shown throughout. To Tim and Rob, your patience throughout this project has been phenomenal, thank you.

To all the trustees of Hope for Justice, thank you so much for your consistent guidance. To Peter, our wonderful chairman, thank you for your wisdom.

Natalie, Stacia, James and Athena, thank you for your part in this story and, more importantly, the vital part you all continue to play in Hope for Justice. I'm so glad we did this! I'm so very proud of what we have achieved and are continuing to achieve together.

I want to say a big thank you to our supporters. These stories of freedom are *your* stories. You really made them happen.

And finally, I want to thank my dog Jessie . . . you (and your barking!) literally get me up every morning.

Prologue

Everybody has a dream. Everybody has something they're passionate about. It might be living in a world free from slavery, it might be mending broken relationships within your family, it might be impacting others through word, song or dance. Everybody has an 'impossible' they hope for. Through this book and the important stories of others held within it, I hope that you discover or reaffirm your 'impossible' and are encouraged to see it for what it is: nothing but a dare.

> Impossible is just a big word thrown around by small men who find it easier to live in the world they've been given than to explore the power they have to change it.
> Impossible is not a fact. It's an opinion.
> Impossible is not a declaration. It's a dare.
> Impossible is potential.
> Impossible is temporary.
> Impossible is nothing.
>
> (Muhammad Ali)

WE
BELIEVE
THERE IS HOPE.

TOGETHER,
WE CAN
END THIS.

Chapter one

WAITING FOR SARAH

There are so many details I remember from that day. The hotel lobby looked so plain, so normal, so everyday: the setting for a thousand meetings. But this meeting was different. I was about to meet a girl we'd rescued from trafficking for sexual exploitation.

I wait quietly, trying to clear my mind, but find I can't stop shuffling in my seat. I check my phone constantly, waiting for the call. My small team has briefed me. Her name was Sarah. She was 19 years old and had spent the past five years trafficked throughout Europe's sex industry. She was forced to work in brothels where men had three to five minutes of her time. She was someone's daughter, raped for profit.

Like many teenage girls, Sarah kept a diary. But instead of filling it with hopes and dreams, she used it to keep count of how many men she was forced to service each day. One day she wrote down the number '117'.

My phone startles me from my thoughts. Our team have collected her safely and are on their way at last. I had thought my role was simple enough but as the moment ticks closer it seems an impossible task: to help this girl believe there's hope where for so long there seemed none; to tell her her nightmare has ended and that she can begin again.

All my preparation for this moment suddenly seems terrifyingly inadequate as I think how empty my words might sound to a girl betrayed. She had been raped, degraded and humiliated. What could I possibly say to restore her faith in humanity?

Time's up. I have to swallow this self-doubt because I've just recognized my team member entering the lobby. Sarah stays at arm's length as she crosses the room. She's wearing a dark tracksuit top over her working attire; only a few hours ago men were wrestling those same clothes from her fragile body. The brothel where she was servicing them is not all that far from here.

I've never seen a person so afraid; terror inhabits every movement she makes. She's gently directed to the seat across from me. She curls up in it, tucking her legs under her chair and wrapping her arms tightly around her chest. She's shaking. Her eyes are darting about. I stop myself from wondering what those eyes must have seen.

We each order a drink and sit in silence until the waitress walks away. Then, quietly, I introduce myself, trying desperately to look reassuring. Sarah says nothing. I start talking about the options for her now, describing the aftercare that's available and the people who can help. Nothing is reaching her. She just stares back, her knuckles white from clenching her drink so tightly that I think she'll shatter the glass. I'm searching for the right words, words that will truly let her know she's safe. I close my eyes, offer a quick prayer and start talking: 'Sarah, we want to put you in a place where you can have your freedom back.'

She lifts her head and looks me full in the face. With lifeless eyes she utters these words so clinically my heart breaks: 'I won't cry.' More words come tumbling out: 'I'll never cry about this. You don't know how it feels. To be abused so badly you can't even walk. You don't know what it feels like to be beaten and raped for years and years. I'll never cry about this. Every day and night I was forced to sleep with fat, old, sweaty men; dribbling and drooling all over me. I have no-one in my life who's there for me. Do you know how bad that is, Ben?' She emphasizes my name as if to say: 'You don't know me.' 'Do you know how that makes you feel? I can never be free from it. Don't tell me I can be free from this.'

I remember to breathe. 'I'm not trying to make you cry', I say. 'What I want to do is tell you that it's over. What was done to you was wrong and we want to put it in the past. We believe there is a future for you; we believe there is hope.' Now that the time has come I can find more words about freedom and fresh starts and life. Gradually her head sinks down, her shoulders start to shake and she begins to cry. The minutes slide by as she sobs, and it's as if the tears of a thousand abuses are released at once. The sobs gradually lessen; she catches her breath, brushes the hair off her damp face, looks up into my eyes and utters the line that changed my life: 'You can call me Emma . . . No-one has called me Emma since this all began.'

STORIES TO SHARE

It's always been a passion of mine. I may not have known the precise path my life would take or that one day I'd find myself sitting in front of Emma, but investing in the next generation has always been important to me. Even as a teenager it was important. That's why, when Mr Stephenson – my secondary school English teacher – gave us a project to write a book for a primary school pupil, my heart leapt. In some ways that was a strange reaction for me. I never really did very well at school. I was always the funny, slightly quirky eccentric kid (I guess some things never change!). I was – and in many ways still am – a bit of an anomaly.

I'm also dyslexic. Words are not my friends. Writing a book seemed a monumental task, even an impossible one. But Mr Stephenson's project gave me an opportunity to invest in someone, a chance to meet with them, hear about their life, their hobbies, their likes and dislikes, and then write a book specifically for them. I was passionate about that part at least! For one of the first times in my schooling history, I was excited. And when I met with my pupil, Sam, this excitement only increased. I left our meeting with my head full of thoughts about what I could do, the story I could tell. The possibilities were endless. I was buzzing. I spent hours and hours on this project – *hours* and *hours*. I crafted each sentence, I planned each paragraph. I even drew some pretty impressive (in my opinion) dinosaurs. There were *lots* of dinosaurs. Everything was neatly coloured, every word carefully chosen. The book was finished. A masterpiece. Or so I thought.

Mr Stephenson called me to his desk. The entire class watched as I beamed with pride, holding my book like a precious stone or regal crown as I approached him. I laid it on the desk. Mr Stephenson studied the cover. He opened the book, and within seconds grabbed his red pen and destroyed me. With every circle, every correction, he announced my failings. As he continued, there was almost a sense of delight as he crossed here, marked there. FAIL. Try again.

I had given everything. I was downbeat but not broken. I went back and took note of Mr Stephenson's corrections, tried to draw better dinosaurs, write more eloquently. You see, I wasn't doing this for me; I was doing this for Sam. The next day I came back with the second edition. The red pen reappeared. The corrections once again began in full flow. I had made new mistakes but hadn't been able to see them. FAIL. Try again. Next came the third edition, then the fourth, the fifth, each one draining more confidence, questioning my abilities, quelling the excitement I'd felt so strongly at the beginning of the process. 'Never again', I thought, promising myself that I wouldn't have another go at writing a book. It was just not in me, not who I am. I'd poured everything into this and failed. It was impossible.

But that's not where the story ends – impossible is not an end, it's a dare. I finished that book because telling Sam's story was worth it. It was painful, it took effort, required patience. And that was just from Mr Stephenson! And here we are again. You are holding another book written by Ben Cooley, except this time there are no dinosaurs.

In 2007 I became aware of human trafficking. Since then I have heard the stories of Emma and Zoe and Khalianna and William, and hundreds of others like them. These stories are not tales of fiction. They are real people with real lives and real families. These stories are not removed or distant, they are taking place today, in our communities. And so, once again, I am pouring everything into this. This time it is not for Sam, it is for them. Just like my childhood self in Mr Stephenson's class refusing to keep Sam's story to myself, I feel I have to write the stories in *this* book because they need to be read.

Since the launch of Hope for Justice in 2008, I have had the pain and the privilege of hearing countless stories of individuals who have fallen victim to modern-day slavery. In the years that have passed we have done things wrong and done things right;

had breakthroughs and breakdowns. But throughout it all it is the stories that sustain us.

'What was done to you was wrong and we want to put it in the past', I had so inadequately tried to tell Emma on that very first meeting. But first she needed to cry. That's why this book exists. Only when we share these stories, acknowledge them and cry out with the victims of modern-day slavery will we be able to make such travesties truly a thing of the past. We believe there is hope. Together, we can end this.

IT'S ALWAYS SOMEBODY'S DAUGHTER.

Chapter two

KHALIANNA'S STORY

Khalianna had trouble at home. Her family was very conservative and restricted what she did and where she went. In and out of arguments, Khalianna decided to move to the city and take care of herself. She would get a good job and prove to her family what she was capable of. She saved just enough money to buy a bus ticket.

On the ride she met another young girl who quickly befriended her. They talked on the way about what they would do when they arrived in the big city. At the last rest stop, Khalianna's new friend offered to jump off and get some drinks. She returned with two bottles of Coke, which they drank.

Unbeknown to Khalianna, the 'friend' had spiked her drink with a sedative that quickly took effect. When they reached the final stop, the 'friend' was met by a group of men who took the now drugged Khalianna back to a hotel. She was repeatedly raped and told that she must make them money by servicing other men.

Khalianna had had a dream to thrive in the city but now that dream had been shattered. Every day she was woken by her trafficker and forced to the room where men arrived to abuse her.

Day after day, hour after hour, minute after minute. Raped, abused, spat on, hair pulled, devalued. She no longer felt human. When the traffickers felt like it, they would abuse her too. It was relentless. Her body no longer felt like her own. Her mind became numb. She looked in the mirror and did not recognize the face looking back. It was gaunt. It was joyless; lifeless.

After months and months of unceasing abuse, Khalianna was rescued. The police had found her and immediately took her to Hope for Justice. There the team loved her, nurtured her and helped her to overcome her trauma and shame.

Over time Khalianna has learned to protect herself and rediscover her future. She now lives in the city, runs her own café and is reconciled with her family. Finally she is free.

PASSION AND PURPOSE

I grew up in the north east of England. I didn't go to university, I went to a conservatoire. Yes, a conservatoire. And no, that's not a glass extension to the back of your house. Not bad for a boy from North Yorkshire! I studied for two years part time and four years full time as an opera singer (a lot of people don't believe this). But believe me I used to wear tights and make-up and dance around. I think one of the main reasons I went into opera was because someone once said I couldn't do it. They said it was the 'highest form of art' and that I couldn't do it. That was all the motivation I needed. I not only attended that place but eventually graduated from it.

During my course I got married to Deb. She was an actress and at that time people would walk up to her in the street and say, 'Hey, you're that girl from the telly.' Kudos to me. I thought it was amazing. We got married quite quickly and although I was still studying, I took various part-time jobs, started a vocal coaching business and got involved in some stage schools. Not long after, the family grew. We had our first child the year I left the conservatoire, when I was 23. We were now a family.

Around that time a couple, Rob and Marion White, joined our church. They were part of a national event called Spring Harvest, and Rob had been National Director for the youth charity, British Youth for Christ. Marion was passionate. She had recently taken up a cause close to her heart, and was so passionate that she wanted to tour the country telling people about it. Perhaps figuring I wasn't busy enough with my vocal consultancy, part-time job, volunteering for the local church and so on, she asked me to help her backstage at an event in Manchester. Requests for favours always fly in when you're at your busiest. Added to the list of responsibilities I was trying to juggle at the time, I was now a husband and had a small child to look after. Life was busy. And yet I knew the very second Marion asked me that it was about to get even busier. It felt to me that supporting the event was something I needed to do. I felt compelled.

Now don't get me wrong: Marion wasn't demanding that I single-handedly orchestrate the event or recruit the team. My job was just to pass the microphones to the speakers, but as the evening began, a video played, detailing Marion's driving passion. It described an issue I had never heard about but would never forget, one that has since become very close to my heart. The video described modern-day slavery. The short film highlighted that 27 million people were held in slavery, that 1.2 million children were trafficked each year; that's two children every minute. Girls like Khalianna and thousands like her. I was blown away; I could not believe it. Statistics can be so overwhelming. Watching from the sidelines, this video changed my understanding of slavery. It was no longer an abstract issue confined to the pages of history. Slavery was alive and well and on my doorstep. The statistics became people. I walked out of Manchester Town Hall that night and thought: 'If that were my daughter I would do something about it.' My next thought changed the direction of my life for ever:

'It's always somebody's daughter.'

I needed to do something.

That night Deb and I lay awake in bed. We couldn't sleep. *We were angry.* Yes, we were angry at the traffickers, but just as angry that this issue was so huge and we had never even heard about it. I felt as if I'd been living in a bubble and was angry at my ignorance. You may not have a particular faith or belief system, but that one short video had challenged my own faith to the core. For me, a person who would describe himself as a Christian, those five minutes of footage shown in Manchester made me question everything. How had we never heard about this issue before?

Both Deb and I had grown up in a largely Christian environment. We'd sat through however many church services and meetings of one kind or another, but for all the church's charitable efforts, it was crazy how few of those occasions had been taken up with this kind of issue. Here is this incredible injustice but few people seemed to be asking 'What can we do about it?' Slavery is an issue that should challenge everybody, not just people in the church. The church is a community that claims to bring light to the darkness and, as churchgoers ourselves, we couldn't help but think: 'If we are not concerned about justice, who is going to be?'

At the time, Deb and I were really involved in leading worship and other creative aspects in our own church. Worship can often be associated with the songs Christians sing in church on a Sunday. But it is so much more than that. To limit worship in this way makes people think that worship is for a certain type of 'worship person'. If you don't go to church you may not know about the worship-leader stereotype. Right now it seems that unless you have an incredible voice and scarily tight skinny jeans to help you reach the high notes, you're not cut out to be a worship leader. But that's nonsense. Worship is for everyone. Whether you have an awful voice or baggy jeans, Christians are called to worship through all areas of their lives. It transcends culture, ability, interests, style and all the other things we've made it into along the way. Sitting awake in bed, unable to sleep, we realized that 'justice' was exactly the same. Justice is one of those issues that has absolutely nothing to do with your personality or your training. Justice isn't something that is for some people, it is for everyone. We couldn't just ignore it.

And so my mind and my spirit were restless, and the questions were no longer just about what I would do about human trafficking. I questioned what life choices I would make. I began reading book after book, getting impacted by the story of Mother Teresa who said, 'Live simply, so others may simply live.' I started making note of quotes such as this from Edmund Burke: 'The only thing necessary for the triumph of evil is for good men to do nothing.' I started hearing from all these people who were passionate about justice, passionate about action, passionate about changing the world.

Something had started to awaken within me. All I had done until now was not enough. This issue would not go away; it followed me around like a shadow. A friend of mine years later told me that he saw within me a 'pure, naive spirit that wanted to change the world'. Everyone I spoke with knew that something had gripped me. Even some of my vocal coaching students had to stop me mid-modern-slavery-flow to ask, 'Do you mind if we do some singing now?' But at this stage, that 'pure and naive spirit', lacked purpose. There was an abundance of passion but no purpose, no plan.

Deb and I had been invited to speak at a conference in Bangor, Northern Ireland. I say 'conference': there were 40 people, so more a weekend away. Even so it was a sell-out, and I wasn't used to writing a message. Nowadays I know people who spend hours and hours preparing this type of talk. They carefully craft each sentence in order to encapsulate the essence of the message they want to get over. Now, through blood, sweat and tears (and many good friends pushing my pen down to paper!), I may have got a bit better at writing a message, otherwise you wouldn't be reading this book. But at that time, that talk, that was just not me. I would write three words. Three. Words. Then I would talk around them.

Deb, on the other hand, was different. She had already prepared her script and, stupidly, I had a look at it before we spoke. It was a couple of days before we were due to do the talks and when I read her message, I was blown away. It was incredible. She had crafted something outstanding. Naturally I'd love to tell you I rushed towards her saying: 'Well done sweetheart' or 'I am so blessed to be married to such a gifted communicator'. I didn't. All I could think was: 'It's better than mine.' In fact it wasn't just better, it was on an entirely different level. Think of Ben & Jerry's Phish Food ice cream. It's amazing: caramel, marshmallows, chocolate – the works. That was Deb's talk. Now think of a bog-standard supermarket value brand ice cream, more ice than cream. That was my talk. The cheap alternative. I had to do something about it.

I got a deckchair and headed to the beach. That might sound like a glamorous solution, but remember this is Northern Ireland! The beach was rocky. And it was cold. Not just normal cold, it was *Northern Ireland* cold. So there I am (with a woolly hat on), and I'm seething, seething at my wife's brilliance! 'Right, Ben', I thought. 'You need a message. A message that will transform people's lives.' Then I thought what I really meant: 'Ben, you need to write a better talk than Debbie's!'

'Help! Help!' Somewhere further down the beach I heard a voice shouting,

'Shut up', I thought. 'I'm trying to write a talk here.'

The voice repeated, 'Help! Help!'

'Shut up', I thought again.

Then it happened. I don't profess to hear the voice of God audibly on a regular basis. In fact this may have been the one and only time in my life. But for me it was at that moment that I heard God say: 'I hope this is not a picture of the church: millions of people trapped in slavery and crying out for help, and you are so bothered about crafting the perfect talk, building a platform and being better than your wife.' You see the Jesus of the Bible is about the poor, about the marginalized, about the oppressed. If Jesus had been sitting on that deckchair and heard the cry of 'Help!', he would have stood up and gone to find that person. He would have gone to give that person peace, love, hope and restoration.

I walked away from the beach that night with an urgency. Not just an urgency to be passionate, to be restless, but an urgency that the church and other communities should be an answer to that voice. It was at that moment that, in my mind, I saw an arena. I had a vision of gathering some friends, of booking an arena and telling the church about modern-day slavery. It was a big vision, and one that for a 26-year-old with very few connections and even less experience would rely on that 'pure, naive spirit' my friend talked about. But as may be clear by now, my mind tends to go to the big places. So when I first saw that arena, I wasn't surprised by its size. I was, however, surprised by its purpose. For one of the first times in my life my 'big idea' wasn't floating on unbridled passion, it was anchored by purpose: a purpose to help people find freedom.

Deb and I came back from Northern Ireland and immediately invited Rob and Marion over for lunch. We couldn't shake the feeling that perhaps if they, with all of their church connections, with all of their years of pastoral leadership and all of the people they've met along the way, could gather all those people, we might be able to inspire them to get involved in this cause. And that together we could make a difference. Perhaps if we had an event and just invited as many churches as would come to rally people, we could inform them, talk to them about the issue, tell them the things that we'd learnt. The issue of human trafficking was so huge, so appalling that it felt too big. But drawing people together to talk about it? That felt within our reach. Talking to Rob and Marion was our next step. They had vast experience of running big events but more importantly, they had incredible wisdom, wisdom we would desperately need if my vision was to become a reality.

I approached Rob and Marion after church and said we'd really like to talk to them about an idea. We invited them round for Sunday lunch and began to share our thoughts. At this point I was feeling pretty relaxed about it all. Usually I'm mildly intense because that's just my nature; in fact the intensity has only increased over the years! But at this point I was relaxed because although

I had had the vision, I thought I would tell them and they would just take it on and I'd have nothing more to do with it. Job done.

'So I've had this vision of an arena', I began.

'What?!', they perhaps unsurprisingly said in reply. Rob and Marion were definitely taken aback. You could see in their faces that what I'd just announced was a surprise. But they were not dismissive.

Together, Deb and I continued: 'You guys have all these contacts and we have this passion for worship, and maybe we can help with that, but what do you guys think about doing something, getting a venue somewhere, having an event in aid of this cause?' We talked about inviting some prominent leaders; talked about inviting people who could bring people not in ones and twos but as a crowd; talked about getting as many people there as possible and then empowering them to go back to their own communities and begin to do something.

'That's an interesting idea, Ben', they said. 'Let's have a think about it and meet again in two weeks.'

Rob and Marion listened to our idea. I mean really *listened*. Rob suggested I put something down on paper, that I clearly present what I thought this could look like. But as you already know, I'm a big-picture guy. I had no idea about how we could make it a reality. First, I thought everyone would do it for free. No-one would want payment, which would be great! We could make some money and we could give it to some of the charities working in the area of human trafficking and that sort of thing. Clearly I had a lot to learn. But time waits for no-one, and two weeks later we were back sitting with Rob and Marion chatting through the idea.

Our two kids were very young at the time, and when I say young I mean Deb had literally given birth to our second daughter a few months before. She was exhausted. And so like any parents, we had to arrange this dinnertime very carefully around their sleep patterns, especially as we wanted to have a serious conversation. So both the kids were asleep, and we had about 45 minutes to have this whole conversation before all hell broke loose.

So there we sat. Ever the optimist, I was fully anticipating that Rob and Marion would agree to organize it and I would go back to my vocal consultancy. They sat down; I gave them their coffees and sat down with mine.

'Yes, we think we should do it', they said.

'Wow', I thought, 'they think we should do it. This is Rob and Marion White, man. *They* think we should do it. That's amazing.'

Then they interrupted my mental fist-pumping with these words:

'But we think *you* should lead it.'

Suddenly my mind filled with a million excuses. I'm not a leader. I'm not capable. I'm just a 26-year-old lad from the north east of England for goodness sake. I'm a dyslexic opera singer, not an event organizer. I wouldn't really even call myself a communicator. It's amazing the excuses that you can come up with in those moments.

I had fully expected Rob to say: 'Right. Thanks for the idea. We'll take it from here. Goodbye', because to some degree that's what I'd tended to see modelled by some of the leaders I'd crossed paths with throughout all streams of life. Not Rob and Marion. This seemingly simple conversation is one of the key times that someone has believed in me and actually modelled true leadership;

one of the times when I saw leadership and thought: 'That is how I would like to be.'

Although I was the kind of kid who liked to prove people wrong, in the two years building up to this moment I'd been so focused on my weaknesses that I'd utterly disqualified myself from doing anything significant. I was sure my motive would probably be wrong, my attitude would be wrong, my character was not right yet. I'd always think that things weren't going to be possible; I'm not going to be able to achieve my goals and my dreams. So even when this vision was deposited in the depths of my soul, I still believed it was someone else's and not mine.

I felt so absolutely empowered when Rob White responded with: 'No, it's yours; go and do it and we'll help you!' Rob, the great leader that he is, was able to see past all the labels I'd put on myself, all my limitations and doubts. He looked past them and just looked for the potential in me: 'Ben, what you have got to realize is that if we waited until we were perfect, no-one would do anything.'

I often wonder whether I would have had the guts to hold on to this vision if they had shut me down in that moment. I was passionate about it, sure. But they were my leaders and I respected them; if they had laughed it off or encouraged me to forget the arena and consider a smaller venue, I sometimes wonder where Hope for Justice would be today.

ANOTHER SIDE TO THE STORY
ROB AND MARION WHITE, CO-FOUNDERS OF HOPE
FOR JUSTICE

It all began on 1 December 2005 when I (Marion) was sitting in a Spring Harvest management meeting in Uckfield, Sussex. A well-known British Baptist minister called Steve Chalke spoke about founding something to be called Stop the Traffik and showed a two-minute video about child trafficking, tracing the children's journey from Africa to the UK. At nearly 60 years old I didn't know anything about human trafficking, but as I saw the immense injustice unfolding before my eyes, I felt a stirring within me: I knew I had to do something. The words that came into my head, clear as day, were: 'You will be like a pebble dropped in a pond; leave me to sort out the ripples.' You may or not believe in a God but, for me, it felt as if it was from him. It was a prompting to do something, an invitation to take a risk.

On my return to Manchester I spoke with my brother, Paul Field, a Christian musician, who amazingly was two months into writing a musical about slavery in the past and in the present day. Over that Christmas I spoke with others in my family about the issue of modern-day slavery, and in the end eight women joined me in a trip to Mumbai in October 2006 to witness for ourselves the massive problem of human trafficking and par-ticularly the work that an organization called Oasis was doing out there in India.

Needless to say, that trip changed my life. Not one of us came back unchanged. Returning to the UK, I knew I had to do something to bring the travesty of human trafficking to the attention of many others who, like me, may have been completely unaware of it. I decided to do a tour of England, together with my brother performing some songs from 'Cargo', the musical he had been working on, and taking the women who had accompanied me to India to put on a multimedia presentation to raise the issue of worldwide human trafficking but particularly here in the UK.

The first venue on our tour was Manchester Town Hall, amazingly given to me free of charge by the Mayor of Manchester. When I spoke at our church about the plans, we asked a number of people to get involved. In particular we were looking for someone to help stage-manage the event in the Town Hall. At 26, trained as an opera singer, Ben Cooley was the best offer we had!

It was clear to us – probably to *everyone* – that Ben had been deeply impacted by what he had seen and heard at the event. And shortly after the tour had finished, he and his wife, Deb, came to see me and my husband, Rob. Ben was passionate about seeing his community – in particular the church – rise up and take a stand against human trafficking. He wanted to book a large venue, preferably Wembley Arena, and call the church to action. Rob and I did try to persuade him to think a bit smaller than Wembley, but in complete faith – or maybe madness! – we booked the NEC in Birmingham for 8 November 2008. The first ripple was happening but it was a bit more like a tsunami!

I (Rob) have been a leader for many, many years; more than I'm going to say! What I love is seeing the potential in people and, if I have the chance, to help that potential develop. I could see Ben's faults (though I won't grass on him!), but I could also see drive, passion and a longing to do something really meaningful. It seemed as if that energy was not being recognized, so when the opportunity came to see that drive and passion released and focused, I counted it a great privilege to get alongside Ben and walk with him through the whole journey of Hope for Justice until now.

People gave me the chances when I was young so I'm a firm believer in getting out of the way and encouraging the next generation. The more that Hope for Justice developed, the less Ben needed to turn to me for help and advice, although in my role as chairman of the board for many years and good friend of Ben's for even longer, we always kept close. So the great thing was that Hope for Justice was not about me but about watching as Ben grew and grew in wisdom and stature. And what a leader he has become! I can still see some faults (I haven't got rid of all of mine!), but what I see in Ben is an innate gift of leadership that operates on many levels. And to what purpose? To seeing many, many victims freed from the prison of slavery and helped to retake their place in society as free men and women.

Those early days of planning our event were a massive adventure. The vision was huge; the arena seemed huge and so the budget was huge! How grateful we were to those who stood with us as we formed a planning group, people such as Viv and Tony Jackson, who stood so closely with us up until recently, and Martin Warner, who still serves on the board. Operation Mobilization helped us to a great extent, as did The Message Trust. We worked so hard at asking people if they could possibly help us through practical hands-on stuff as well as financially, and many responded so generously. The final cost for the event was near to £250,000 and, as we drove into the NEC car park on 7 November, we realized that if people didn't turn up the only collateral we had was our house! It was a scary thought but it was one we had to embrace. We believed in the event. We believed in Ben, but more importantly we believed in the heart behind it and in what the soon-to-be-named Hope for Justice was longing to achieve.

MAY HE JUDGE YOUR AFFLICTED ONES WITH JUSTICE.

Chapter three

TOBIAS AND ELENA'S STORY

Tobias and his wife Elena saw what looked like some great job opportunities online. As a result, they applied for the roles and moved with their family to the UK. When they arrived with their young children, the accommodation they had been promised turned out to be squalid and totally unacceptable for kids. The smell was overwhelming, the walls were dirty, the rooms were dark and the place had barely any furniture inside.

During their first day working in their new jobs, Tobias and Elena quickly realized that what they thought was a legitimate opportunity, what they thought was a chance to better their family and build for their future, was in reality something very different. Soon they were treated like animals.

After working for four weeks, both Tobias and Elena were paid just £5. Five pounds to feed their entire family. For their family's sake they decided to leave, but try as they might they could not find alternative work. Every possible avenue closed. They became desperate, to the point where they felt they had no choice but to return to the same 'franchise' run by their trafficker, which had various jobs across the country.

They were soon given work to do, but the unreasonable 'expenses' deemed by the trafficker to be legitimate grew into a 'debt' to their employer. The debt spiralled; their captors became increasingly violent. They demanded to be repaid, but with so little income this was impossible. They were trapped. Physical and verbal abuses were continual; Tobias and Elena were pushed, punched and shouted at, until one day Tobias was stabbed.

Sitting in hospital, Tobias had every reason to fear further reprisals. Too terrified to make a formal police complaint, he felt compelled to return to their life of exploitation. Two months later the family were reached by the frontline service of an organization trained by Hope for Justice. Its team had been trained in how to spot the signs and to identify such situations and called in our experts.

When we met them, Tobias and Elena had nothing but their children and a few possessions in their arms. Hope for Justice arranged for immediate safe accommodation and worked to meet the family's most pressing needs, including a good meal and plenty of milk for their smallest child.

Tobias and Elena had experienced year after year of fruitless labour, debt and violence. They had been promised a dream that fast became a living nightmare. But now they are free and starting to build the life they deserve.

GATHERING MOMENTUM

Over the following months, Rob and Marion introduced me to a load of people. I travelled up and down the country sharing the vision of what we wanted to do. I was so naive. But in some ways, these days laid the foundation for the man I would become. The vision was gaining momentum, the excitement was contagious. Very quickly we started building a team of people in support of the project. People were meeting people, introducing them to me, sharing the vision, sharing the passion. We were getting some incredible people on board, such as Rob Allen.

At the time, Rob was working for a major multinational organization and overseeing budgets of hundreds of millions of pounds. We asked him if he could help with the finances for the event. Of course he could! He was handling budgets far bigger than ours. But he wasn't captivated by the figures; he was captivated by the vision. And there were other great individuals who wanted to support us, such as Chris Dacre.

I think that was probably the first time I was really nervous about meeting someone who would later become a member of our team. As I sat waiting to have tea with Chris, I couldn't help but think the same thought over and over: he lives in a different world from me. I knew about tights and make-up; he knew about ledger lines and commercial property! But as soon as he arrived it became apparent that we did have one very key thing in common. Chris has always been passionate about the abolition of sex trafficking. When we started talking it was clear he felt really strongly that he needed to do something to fight against this evil. We shared the same hope, the same vision. Then Chris introduced me to another guy who would soon become an important part of the Hope for Justice story: Tim Nelson.

When we first decided to put on this event, a lot of people were quite impressed by the size of our ambitions. Tim was the first person I met along the journey who thought: 'Well, what we need to do is make it bigger! We need to do it better! We need to push this to another level!' And I thought I was a big thinker! When I would eventually go to hire the arena, the original quotes were as much as £80,000; I'd spent a lot of time managing to get this down to about £40,000 after much toing and froing and many meetings. I was preparing to go to the board with great anticipation of them giving me a round of applause and hearty congratulations. Before I could announce my achievement, Tim spoke to me and said: 'I bet we could get it for £10,000.' What?! So then the board sent me back to ask if we could have it for even less. That's Tim Nelson! He's got this unbelievable belief in the good of humanity, even in the face of evidence that shows otherwise. Everyone needs a Tim Nelson in their world. Yes, you need people to tell you stone cold facts, but you also need someone to pull you up into a different way of thinking. And sure, I didn't get it for £10,000. But you know what? Tim inspired me and pushed me on, and we all need someone like that in our lives.

Tim Nelson is also the guy who decided what our event would be called; well, he and a small Anglican church called St Andrews! Tim had heard about this church and that they were running a small youth event, getting ten or twelve people together on a Friday night. They were calling this event The Stand. The name clearly had an impact on him. Soon he started telling me how he thought it would be an amazing name for a much bigger event and that maybe we could use it for ours. It made sense. We weren't just gathering people to raise awareness; we wanted to prompt action. We wanted people to do something. We could ask them to take a stand, to take The Stand against slavery. It was perfect. The Stand wasn't just an ethereal name for an event; it was actually something that would mean something to people.

Not content with naming our event, it was also Tim who would later come up with the name for our organization. In the same year we launched there was an initiative called Hope 08 launching. Tim thought it would be a great idea to tie in with that.

But we didn't want to be hope. We wanted to hope *for* something. Justice was the thing we wanted to see and so Hope for Justice was born.

With Chris and Tim and many other exceptionally talented individuals getting on board, the momentum was growing. I had a vision of an arena and now – excitingly, scarily, unbelievably – more and more people were beginning to share that vision too.

Initially I didn't know which arena we would fill. We didn't originally pick the NEC and, actually, the first time I was really hit by what we were trying to do was when I walked round another arena, in Manchester. It was huge, this massive open space. Obviously, being an opera singer I couldn't resist letting out a bit of Verdi; the acoustics were fantastic! But I'll never forget the moment when the manager said that in order to hire this building, for the numbers we were talking about, we would actually need to bring in our own toilets. It was another detail I hadn't imagined, but sure, fine: we'd bring our own toilets if we had to. What was that going to be? A couple of hundred quid? Nope. Not even close, more like £30,000. 'Maybe we don't need toilets after all', I thought. 'Perhaps we could just ask them to hold it in or go beforehand.' That was my 'fear' moment; that's when I realized what we were doing. Up to that point it felt as if we were building up to do a really big PowerPoint presentation. It wasn't until I walked round the arena that I thought: 'Ah, this is actually quite big. This is why not many people do this!' But we'd come too far to go back now.

And so after weeks of travelling and speaking across the UK, gathering a growing number of people to share the vision for an event that would allow us to tell the hidden stories of slavery, I had abruptly remembered that it was time to book the arena. Dialling the number of the NEC Arena in Birmingham – the seventh-largest exhibition centre in Europe – I waited for someone to pick up the phone. And then they did.

'Hi, my name is Ben Cooley and I would like to book the arena please,' I said.

'OK, sir. Where are you from?'

'Originally, the north east of England but now I live in Manchester.'

There was a long pause on the end of the line.

'No, sir,' the voice on the phone finally broke the silence, 'I meant which company are you from?'

'Oh, I need a company?' I said, 'I'll write that down.'

Clearly I knew nothing about booking, organizing or hosting an event. The conversations I had with the sound and lighting guys, for example, were equally hilarious:

'I need sound and lighting for an arena,' I said to them. The guy who worked there emailed me a quote. I felt a little bit sick and then I rang him up: 'I'm really sorry man; I didn't want to buy the equipment. I only just wanted to rent it for the day.'

I was met with the same long pause.

'That is the day rental cost, Ben.'

Putting on this event was not going to be a walk in the park!

From that moment all the prices and numbers we were talking about, the figures being thrown around, the cost of this and the cost of that, all seemed so beyond our reach. Each time another matter was mentioned I'd think 'Damn, really?!' I really didn't have the first idea about the practicalities of hiring a huge venue like this or even about getting people to come.

And for all the support we received, for all the encourage-ment, there were the ones who thought we were crazy. Many people would make throwaway comments like: 'You know no-one will go to that kind of thing?' 'It's a waste of time organizing it!', 'Who's going to travel from Manchester to Birmingham?' You know, as if it were the furthest distance you could imagine!

'It's less than two hours away! Why would anyone not care enough?' Deb would say to me. I didn't know either. Maybe it was naivety, maybe it was ignorance, but we just thought: 'It's important; of course people will come!' In those moments we believed with a childlike faith that people would come. As a Christian, I believe the Bible when it says that God uses the foolish things of this world to confound the wise. And it's a good job too, because in those moments we didn't have a clue!

After I'd finally plucked up the courage to book the arena, we had another setback. The arena had received a counter-booking offer and so to secure the date they needed our deposit, and fast. Suddenly we had to provide thousands of pounds of deposit or we were going to lose the venue. There was nothing in our bank accounts. We had no chance. And no way to raise that kind of money personally. Humbly, we had to approach anyone we could think of who might just have that kind of money to spare. I made some phone calls, asked some people. And do you know what? Most of the people I expected to say 'yes' said 'no'. And then the money came in, just when we needed it, from a completely unexpected source.

You see, we were trying to get people to buy into a vision. That's hard for any organization, even long-established ones. In many cases these organizations that have been around for a while build on the reputation of what they did before. It turns out that when you set up an organization, you don't usually set it up with a large event. No, you set it up small, and you build and build so that you can turn to people for support and say: 'Look, this is what we've done in the past; this is what we want to do in the future. Do you want to get involved?' So more individuals tend to get involved as you go along.

With The Stand we were asking people to trust us from the start. We had no record of what we had done in the past but we were asking people to support our future. Instead of gathering enough cups of water together to fill a basin, it was like turning on a tap and expecting it to flow to fill a large pool. With The Stand we were saying 'No, we're going to go big and we're going to go hard, and if it goes wrong that's that!' So The Stand was a risk, but one many of us were willing to take.

ANOTHER SIDE TO THE STORY
TIM NELSON, INTERNATIONAL DEVELOPMENT DIRECTOR,
HOPE FOR JUSTICE

I was out for dinner in Los Angeles when the guy I was with told me how he had seen young girls trapped in cages in India with his own eyes. I was disgusted that such injustices were still taking place. 'You know this is going on in your city as well?' he said. And then he challenged me, 'What are you prepared to do about it?'

I had first heard about the issue through my friend Chris Dacre, who was passionate about doing something about the problem of trafficking. So when I came back from the USA, I challenged him further on it. Soon he was telling me about a trained opera singer called Ben Cooley who was trying to put on a major event to raise awareness about the issue. 'Maybe you could help him?' he said.

When I first met Ben I instantly loved his vision and passion. I also loved his naivety. He just gets so caught up in the fact that 'We've *got* to make a difference!' From that moment on I was in.

I'd done events for my church before, had run host teams and welcome teams, but I'd never started something from scratch. Together Ben and I started to get more and more people on board. Ben, Deb, Rob and Marion worked so hard. We knew we needed to get people to commit to bring coachloads rather than just ones and twos to make it happen. We were doing the best we could with the small team we had. We'd all pulled in friends and family to try and help where we could, and most of us didn't live anywhere near Birmingham!

We'd certainly set ourselves a challenge. But I think when you're going to do something like an event, the real challenge is not in the launch (because people are excited). It's not in the actual event itself (because then you're in the moment). The biggest challenge for me came when we were six months into planning and hadn't had as many people booking tickets as we'd have liked. Your stomach drops and you think: 'What are we going to do?!' It happens time and time again. Six months in, the temptation is to pull back, change your strategy, cancel, do something different because to carry on as normal will mean being left with egg on your face. Not Ben. Ben was the kind of gung-ho guy who would say: 'I don't care. I feel like this is what we should do. We have got to make this happen!' That kind of zeal, that kind of passion, is a challenge; it's something people feel they want to get involved in. I think people could see that authenticity in what we were trying to do with The Stand. Here was an event that wasn't led by a well-known Christian leader, but an unknown group prepared to take on something colossal. But Ben didn't want to take it on alone. Good leaders want to include you in their mission; great leaders want to share it with you.

This is something that has remained with me since my involvement in The Stand right up until today. I've had the immense privilege to be on the founding board of the charity and serve on the board until I was able to step full time into working at Hope for Justice as International Development Director. Hope for Justice is about a shared vision, it is about fighting for something together. When you can stop saying 'they' about Hope for Justice and you move to saying 'we', it changes everything. It shifts from being an outside organization to being one that is inclusive. I would say the same for churches, for businesses, for individuals. When people realize that it's 'we' together rather than 'they', then you realize it doesn't matter who gets the credit.

I've had the privilege of seeing kids who are willing to give every single penny of their pocket money to make a difference, mums who are giving up on luxuries they could have in their household to help bring freedom. I see the commitment from so many who are prepared to get up early, bake cakes for a bake sale or train so they can do a charity walk, all to further 'our' mission. It never fails to inspire me how individuals train for a year to be able to run a marathon or give up every spare moment outside of working to help organize a group fundraising event. These are the real modern-day heroes who go the extra mile doing all they can to help. These people are so inspiring. I met a chap who couldn't walk who was prepared to go on his mobility scooter on a massive journey, one where he would be in a lot of pain: it was so long that he had to get off and change his battery!

I cannot shake the fact that just a number of meetings – a few meetings with the right individuals – can lead to determination and action that set people free. When I was a kid, my mum always gave me dot-to-dot puzzles to do. I could never work them out: '1' was so far away from '2' and then suddenly the '3' was right beside it. The whole time you don't quite understand what you're drawing; it's only when you step back that you see the full picture. I think the same could be said for the fight against slavery. You meet with one person who is connected to a person in a different place, who connects you with his or her friend, and suddenly you start to see a pattern emerging that leads to people being set free, that leads to a picture of the end of slavery in a country. It's that dot-to-dot, and it's happening all over the world, all at the same time.

FOR AS
HE THINKS IN
HIS HEART,
SO HE IS.

Chapter four

AMAYA'S STORY

Amaya was 14 when she was tricked into working at a Cambodian brothel. She was forced to service ten men a day, endured beatings and gang rapes and became addicted to drugs. She was treated, she said, as if she wasn't human. She was a slave.

Since she was a little girl, Amaya had dreamed of having a good job and earning money to help her mother. She had dreamed of having a hair salon and becoming a pop singer. But after her birth father had passed away and her mother had remarried, Amaya needed to work day and night to earn money to provide for the family. Her family life went downhill. Sometimes they had nothing at all to eat. Amaya felt such a deep sense of disappointment. She was disappointed with her situation, her family unity, her life. She had so many questions. Why did her life turn from bad to worse? Why was her family situation so hopeless? They had no money even though they worked so hard.

One day a relative of Amaya's was drunk. He raped her. She felt angry and afraid. During that time she kept the rape a secret. She was full of shame and did not know how to explain it to anyone. She could not tell her mother what had happened and was so ashamed she went to live with a friend. Then that friend brought Amaya to work in a place without telling her what kind of job it was: Amaya was taken to a brothel.

Previously Amaya had thought her life was in as bad a place as it could possibly be, but now she felt more depressed than she had ever thought possible. One day a group of clients raped Amaya in a graveyard. They took turns to abuse her, taking great delight in their carnal gratification. Once they had finished with her limp body, they left her alone. She was not allowed time to rest or recover, but was forced to return to work to service customers, one after another, only a few minutes each time. She cried as her 'customers' abused her.

Amaya felt her life was like a doormat for others to step on and use as they liked. But then things changed. A group of police officers came to rescue her and many other exploited girls. Despite being their rescuers, they spoke to the girls with no respect at all, calling them 'bitches' and making them feel like scum. After Amaya was rescued by the police she was referred to Hope for Justice and began her rehabilitation programme.

Amaya worked through her trauma and began healing from the pain of her past. She began to discover a new dream for her future. When she was brought to Hope for Justice, for the first time in many, many years she felt excited. She felt happy. She was now in a family-like atmosphere that made her feel warm, loved and valued.

Graduating the Hope for Justice programme, Amaya went on to become a licensed yoga instructor and now works with 'at risk' children. She is happily married and has a young child.

WELCOME TO MUMBAI

It was the smell that hit me first. I had never encountered such a smell. And such humidity. The air was sticky, thick and hot. Welcome to Mumbai.

It was my first ever long-haul flight. I'd never been outside the developed world before and had no idea what to expect. This country was like nothing I had ever seen. It was crazy. There were cars, people and animals everywhere. It was absolutely manic. A motorbike passed me with a goat on the back. *A goat!* In the UK that could make the news; in India it was just another Monday!

It was Marion White who had put me in touch with a contact in India. He was one of the members of the event's board and had agreed to pay for me to visit some projects set up to fight slavery. Here I had the incredible opportunity to meet some of the amazing individuals fighting modern-day slavery. These people became heroes to me and humbled me; they weren't just raising awareness, they were getting people out. They were rescuing. From the top lawyers to talented investigators, this team was actually 'doing the stuff' and doing it with such incredible professionalism. I looked at these people and I thought: 'This is it.' Suddenly I was seeing sustainable mechanisms for rescue; seeing effective methods to address rule of law; seeing people who could bring more than awareness. People who could bring *freedom*. Those two weeks in India were life changing. It was then I realized that the focus of our passion should be not just for an event but for a movement.

I spent every day leaning in, asking questions:

Why do you do it like this?
How do you do it like this?

How do you do investigations?

How do investigations sit within the law of the land?

What does it feel like when you do a rescue?

How do you build a sustainable team?

I was up all night, reading and thinking of more questions:

How do you deal with the constant bombardment of negativity?

How do you cope with the darkness and oppression of the world of slavery?

How do you maintain a spirit of hope?

How do you keep your team motivated?

How do you keep your staff safe?

The questions just kept coming:

How do you face children who have been exploited in this way?

How do you break down criminal syndicates?

How do you as an NGO relate to government agencies?

How do you get your funding?

Is your funding sustainable?

Do you worry about your funding?

Does that affect your growth?

How would you use $1 million to expand your work?

What's the relationship between rescue and restoration?

How does that impact prosecutions?

How do you make sure it's not just Mumbai?

How do you affect the infrastructure of a nation?

Is what you are doing replicable?

I didn't know where these questions were coming from but I had once been told that the best leaders ask the best questions. And so two weeks of question after question – early morning to late at night – I listened for their answers and tried to soak up their wisdom. I was exhilarated; they, on the other hand, were exhausted. Then one day, after I had asked every question I could think of, they turned to ask me one: 'Ben, do you want to see it?'

Ever since I had been made aware of the problem of human trafficking in that meeting in Manchester Town Hall, I had become incredibly passionate about the issue. But for some reason I had never thought I would see it first hand. Even when I went to India, I was going in order to understand the cause in more detail, to ask questions and support organizations like these guys who were doing incredible work. Perhaps it was my naivety again, but I didn't think they'd ever ask me if I wanted to *see* it. And now that they had, everything in me wanted to say 'no'. But I knew in my heart the answer was 'yes'.

We meet in a coffee shop not far from central Mumbai. I'd been told by a member of our team to pose as a paedophile. The guy who meets us is one of our guys, but he has built up a rapport with some of the local pimps. We get in the car together. There are three of us. It's night time. The air is sticky. Then the pimp gets in.

He is going to find us children. I hear him talking. The things I hear him say are some of the most horrendous words I have ever heard. For the first time I am meeting someone who not only thinks it is all right to abuse children, but makes his living from it. He profits from their pain, he profits from their abuse.

I am calm but conflicted. He takes us to this brothel. The building looks awful. There are huge steel doors. No light. It's a warehouse. Nothing to suggest what goes on inside. People simply walk by. Opposite us is another really old run-down building, another one people just walk past. But suddenly I hear music coming from it. The more it plays, the more I recognize it. 'Did you feel the mountains tremble?' The words rang out: they were playing a Delirious? song. The unassuming building across from us is a church!

We turn back to our building and the rusted brothel doors open. I don't get scared easily; I'm usually pretty self-assured. But in this moment, fear sets in. I'm not scared for my life; I'm scared of the unknown. I didn't know what was behind the door. As much as the team in India has told me, no-one could describe what it felt like in reality. No-one could explain the monstrosity of human trafficking in words.

Suddenly panic sets in, and not just for me. Our undercover operative seems to panic. The pimp begins to panic. They have let us in too early. There is a policewoman ahead of me. My mind is racing. 'What happens next?' I think. 'Are we going to get arrested? Are we going to jail? How will we explain this to the police?'

But the policewoman isn't there to administer justice. She is there to accept her weekly bribe. That was the first moment I sensed injustice. Justice means the correct use of power and authority. Injustice is the exact opposite. That policewoman had the power and authority to make a difference, but she was misusing that for her own benefit. Suddenly the enormity of human trafficking became all the more real. We were standing in a place where we could buy a child.

We are taken to a room. The metal door slams behind us and the steel bolt shook me as it locked. We have nowhere to run. No way of getting out. A woman is talking to our operative, part in English, part in Hindi. I can't understand it all. We are led out of that room into a more presentable one. We all sit down on this L-shaped sofa. Then the pimp starts asking me questions: 'What type of girl do you want? How old you want her to be?' He uses language that makes my skin crawl. The way he is describing the girls to be revealed is disgusting. Interrupting his questions, a woman comes in and offers us drinks. But I don't want a drink; it's the last thing I want right now. Next she informs us that she doesn't have any young girls who match our criteria, not because she doesn't have any in the building but because they are with other men. She offers us some alternative girls. Would we be interested in looking at them? Would we like to see them? Once again, though everything in me is screaming no, the answer given is a simple yes.

The L-shaped sofa is at the back of the room. Directly in front of me is a door, and the door leads to a hallway. Above us are corridors and corridors leading to room after room of broken, vulnerable, abused girls. The woman stands at the door. There is a cord next to her that I hadn't noticed until that moment. She pulls the cord and a bell rings somewhere in the distance, somewhere down the corridors. She pulls the bell several times, almost as if it were a code dictating which type of girl should come out. And within a matter of minutes, two girls arrive at the door.

Stunned and petrified, I sit motionless on the sofa. I am thousands of miles away from home and I am not expecting the girls in front of me to be the same. They walk into the room and I can barely contain my shock. They are white. They are European.

And they are young. I am sitting in a brothel in one of the metro cities of India and suddenly the reality dawns on me: this is a global issue. Women are being trafficked to every corner of the world to cater for the screwed-up, perverted tastes of men who want to buy them, abuse them and degrade them. I look into the eyes of the girls standing before me. The eyes looking back at me are not just sad; they are empty. They are hopeless.

Everything in me wants to tell them: 'It's going to be all right. We're going to get you out of here. There is hope.' But I can't. At that moment the woman at the door pulls another cord and a light suddenly comes on the girls. They start spinning. The woman asks: 'Do you like these girls? Do you want to have them?' Disguising our disgust, we both say 'No', make our excuses and leave.

Standing in the street, my body goes into shock. My mind cannot focus. It's almost as though I'd experienced a trauma. Our host asks us if we want to visit another brothel. Tears had begun welling up in my eyes. 'No', I say through tears, 'I never want to enter another brothel until I know I can get them out. I don't want to see any more girls and have to leave them.' I don't want any of those girls to remember my face as just another face that saw them as a piece of meat with no value.

That experience repulsed me to my very core: as a father, as a husband. It was awful.

That night I couldn't sleep. I called Deb and could hardly speak through the tears. I left the television on all night just to fill the silence. That was the moment that I knew that seeing an end to modern-day slavery had turned from being a spasm of passion to a lifelong mission. Slavery once again had a face. Slavery was those two girls.

ANOTHER SIDE TO THE STORY
PETER STANLEY, FORMER STRATEGY DIRECTOR
AT STOP THE TRAFFIK

I first heard about The Stand while I was working for Stop the Traffik, a global coalition united in the mission to help stop the sale of people, see traffickers prosecuted and protect the victims of modern-day slavery. After hearing about a team from Manchester who had travelled to India to serve with our organization, I decided to pay them a visit. As I met the leader of the group, Marion White, I also encountered Ben and Deb Cooley.

I will never forget meeting the larger-than-life character that is Ben for the first time. He was so pumped with energy. More than that, he wanted to focus it. I knew he just needed the right direction and he would be off. Long before the name Hope for Justice was coined, he had a great group of people around him and was ready to take on the world.

After that first meeting it wasn't long before it struck me: I had been talking so much about human trafficking but never actually seen it in reality. I knew Ben was the same. And so my wife Gillie and I arranged with Oasis India to visit their team, and we invited Ben to join us. Needless to say, he didn't need any persuading.

Our first experience of India had a huge impact on us as we saw the vast slums through the plane windows and as we stepped outside the airport into the crazy traffic, which was complete mayhem. Our first night was in a 'businessmen's hotel' but it was still a long way from what we had expected. Ben was up half the night unable to shut out the noise of dogs barking loudly and incessantly outside his window.

The time we spent with the multidisciplinary rescue team was inspiring. They were dedicated and professional. And their stories were extraordinary: of secret compartments to hide children; of corrupt police; of the vast numbers of prostitutes in the huge red-light districts. Towards the end of our time with the team, Ben and I were handed a challenge. We were told that one of the agents was posing as a recruiter of sex tourists so that he could gain access to brothels and see where there was illegal child prostitution and trafficking. He was a church pastor who had decided to risk his life to fight trafficking. And then the team leader asked Ben and me if we would join the man on a visit to a brothel the following night. He said we were free to say no. It was meant as a challenge. He warned us that we would probably be locked in and there were likely to be firearms. So we had to sleep on it and decide whether we were up for it or not. It was difficult, but we already knew the answer.

The next day we agreed to visit the brothel that night. We were to pose as sex tourists looking for 'fresh young girls'. The idea was to see if we could help our agent friend locate any underage trafficked children. When the time came we got into a taxi and were driven to meet the pimp who would take us to the brothel. So we met the pimp and drove further into Mumbai. Then he told us that the police had raided the brothel the night before and he was taking us somewhere else across town. The safety car, who had been following us for protection, lost us. We were on our own. We eventually got to a grotty side street where we were told to wait on the curb for our turn to enter the brothel. The lasting impression was sickening. The madam was a cheery little grandma who gave the impression nothing was amiss as she offered us a glass of water and made conversation while the girls came down. We felt totally fake. It seemed obvious that we weren't sex tourists. And yet nobody noticed. It was a scary moment but we prayed under our breath and kept faith in what we were called to do. We had been told beforehand that some agents had been attacked and forced to use the girls when they were found out. So we sat on the sofa, as two Eastern European girls stood before us, under the fluorescent light. There was no allure, nothing sexy, no glitz; simply a 'Do you want me or not?' Our experience was one of a meat market, a transaction, an impersonal recreation for men to get their nightly relief. It was sickening and dark.

Though it is not enough, until we see the end of slavery, organizations like Hope for Justice and Stop the Traffik shed some light in this dark place. I know Ben, Deb and their team have used the India model of cooperation to real effect in the UK, and I know the energy that I first saw in Ben remains to this day.

NOTHING EXTRAORDINARY THAT HAPPENS IN THIS WORLD COMES WITHOUT A COST.

Chapter five

Jared had brought £100 with him to the UK. He had resolved to live on that for four weeks while he looked for work. He had always worked. He knew the value of working hard and contributing to society. Now he wanted to work in the UK and pursue the dreams he had for his life.

After four weeks he was offered a job. He was delighted. It wasn't the ideal job but it was a start and he could see it would give him a springboard from which to better himself. Unbeknown to him, the job was offered to him by a trafficker.

The trafficker told Jared that the job was to be processed through an agency and all his salary was to be paid directly into its bank account. Jared, who didn't speak any English, never saw the card or papers for this account.

Not long after that he received a letter stating that there was a debt on this account, more than he could ever repay. He was completely dumbfounded: he had never used the account. He was desperate. Jared worked for ten hours a day, six days a week, sometimes seven days a week. He was moved from place to place, he slept in the kitchen at one house and in the lounge at the next. Often, his abusers would hit him and slap him.

On one occasion Jared tried to escape. He thought he had made it, but that hope was dashed and the traffickers eventually caught him and beat him heavily. They took his documents to stop him attempting to run away again.

Jared didn't trust the police. In his home country, most of the law enforcement officers were corrupt and often acted as criminally as those on the wrong side of the law. He didn't know if he could trust the police in the UK. He did think about approaching them but the trafficker knew his family and Jared didn't want to put them in any danger. His family had no idea what had happened to him. He hadn't been able to contact them because he didn't have their phone number, and had no idea whether the traffickers had told lies about him or his whereabouts.

Jared managed to find the strength to keep going. The beatings were difficult. The abuse was continual. Day by day he could feel himself losing hope, losing strength and losing the will to live. And that's when Hope for Justice found him. After years of hell, Jared was identified and rescued by Hope for Justice's specialist team. He was eventually taken to a place of safety where he began to rebuild his life, his confidence and his trust in others.

TAKING THE STAND

The congregation was silent. I had only been asked to talk, to share a little of our story, for two minutes, but here I was finishing off this story twenty minutes later. Since returning from India I had continued travelling up and down the country speaking to people, to churches, sharing the vision we had for The Stand. Yes, my visit had made me understand that the mission had to be much bigger than one conference, one event; but we had to start somewhere, and the arena event was it. Sharing the stories of people like Jared and Emma and Amaya, individual after individual, leader after leader, church after church began to understand what we were trying to do. They were fully in. This was not just my vision; this was now our vision, and we needed all the support we could get.

As I've mentioned previously, the organization of an arena event is not easy. For a team of ten or fifteen people it would be a challenge. For us, it was me with the help of a handful of others. And though our passion and purpose were strong, the practicalities of it were becoming a strain.

In the lead-up to The Stand, I remember going with Deb to another event at the NEC Arena. I walked in and took a deep breath. Wow, there were a lot of seats. It was a big place. Deb could see it was a big place. Everyone could see it was a big place. And yet I still made a point of looking up and down the aisle and telling Deb: 'If we're going to break even we're going to have to fill up to this point. The seats are going to have to be filled up to here in order to make the money we need.' In those kinds of moments it's hard not to think: 'What do we do if people don't come?' But we couldn't allow ourselves to think like that. Only a few of the team involved with The Stand owned their own properties, and they were potentially set to lose them if this didn't work. So emotionally, physically and mentally, putting on The Stand was stretching us. I was still doing my day job as a vocal consultant, and with the pressure of organizing the event was working all hours of the day and night. It was just becoming too much. Then Deb lost her job.

I knew we needed help, so I turned once again to Rob White. We discussed our situation and he agreed that something needed to change and that really I should be working full time on the event. In some ways this meant we were forced into a place where now we were living by faith. It was the only option if we were to see the vision become a reality. When I say living by faith, we literally didn't know how we might pay the bills each month. I don't have an extravagant lifestyle, but I remember that there was an occasion when I just wanted my kids to have swimming lessons. So I booked them. Then Chris Dacre – now a member of our board – came around to our house one day to help us with our family budgeting, and told me that we simply couldn't afford the lessons. So we had to cancel them. It was like a punch in the stomach. I was devastated, knowing we didn't have enough money. My Dad had worked for an insolvency company so I had seen the dark side of debt and was desperate not to be in it. My kids were 3 years old and 1 year old. We needed to provide for them first. We didn't buy Christmas presents for the kids until they were 7 years old. I started skipping lunches so the family could eat. Then I skipped breakfasts. I wouldn't recommend this as a course of action but I felt it was the only way to survive.

One day I attended a conference. There was a place where a number of leaders were meeting, and I was invited to join them. The lunch provided was a self-service buffet. I was hungry and there was an abundance of food on offer. Naturally, I filled my plate. At that point one of the leaders shouted across to me: 'Where there's a free dinner, there's always Ben Cooley.' They meant it as a joke but it broke me. I didn't respond physically, but inside I felt so small. I didn't blame them. They didn't know I hadn't eaten all day, didn't know I hadn't eaten much that week, but for the next few days I couldn't get it out of my mind. I felt stupid and embarrassed. It hurt. And yet it taught me a valuable lesson: words have power. It has made me really careful about speaking into people's lives. Throwaway, frivolous jokes can have a far deeper impact than intended.

Organizing The Stand cost us. But nothing extraordinary that happens in this world comes without a cost, and in many ways, despite the hardship, these were some of the best days of my life. I realized then that being comfortable does not enrich my soul. Even though I was hungry, I had never felt so clearly that I was doing exactly what I had been made to do. I was right in the middle of my calling. Material things became so insignificant to me. Yes, I wanted to provide for my family. Yes, I wanted the best for my children. But even though we had so little in those days, in many ways I have never felt so rich.

There were just two weeks to go until The Stand, and I'd recently been told that we'd pretty much sold all of our tickets. What's more, despite my personal struggles I was now feeling confident about the conference's finances; we were going to break even. But as so often with many of us, I was on to the next worry: the logistics. I was petrified. We had organizations and people to help us, we had volunteers; but there are things you just don't think about when you've never organized an event. Such as hospitality.

Through the help of Tim Nelson we managed to pull in a few favours from some people he knew musically who could come and play at the event. We approached the musician Tim Hughes and Switchfoot frontman Jon Foreman, as well as a number of other performers, to come across from the USA. The musicians flew into the UK and I had thought they could just get a taxi from the airport to our venue. False. Their team asked me who was picking them up. I had limited options. So my Dad went to pick up the Grammy award-winning, platinum-selling bands from the

USA in his Renault Megane. With the kids' car seats still in the back!

I remember another one of the artists asking me: 'Is there any water?'

'There's water in the tap.' I thought, before we sent someone to a local supermarket to get some bottled water. I was oblivious then but now I see that there is great value in these things. These guys are on the road all the time, and far from demanding, these little touches really do help them do their job better. I didn't mean to dishonour them in any way, I simply didn't know. No-one had told me how you did these things. I was responsible for everything and I was learning on my feet.

★ ★ ★

The day finally arrives and I am trying to prepare for my big speech. This is the fourth time I have spoken publicly at an event. My fourth time and there are 5,884 people in the audience. This is serious, man. I am nerv-ous!

About an hour before I'm due to take the stage, I'm standing by the side of the platform, holding my speech notes, practising my lines, when one of our volunteers comes up to me. He has a problem and I go to help him sort it out. When I get back to the stage I'm looking for my notes. They're not here. Where are they?! I've lost my speech. I can't find my notes. I panic. Breathing deeply, I have to go on stage without them. I'd been so consumed with preparing this event that I simply hadn't had time to learn my speech. But with the notes long gone, I have no other option: I have to speak from the heart. I look out. Thousands of people are filling this great arena. I begin to speak, the words are coming, I am in full flow. Then I notice that the first five rows are empty. My heart sinks: 'Wasn't I meant to fill them?' I think to myself while 5,000 or so eyes gaze on: 'They were meant to be for the special guests.' Catching my breath, I see them on the very back row. 'Darn it, they were meant to be at the front.' Silencing my thoughts, I get back on track, sharing the message, sharing the stories. As I finish my talk and walk off the stage, I feel terrible. Not because of the seats and not because of the logistics but because I am finally on the comedown.

The momentum had been non-stop for the past few months building up to the event. There was a crescendo and peak of energy delivering the talk, and then it changed. I've been told that a lot of leaders, preachers and public speakers feel this. There's a real low following any event. I'd spoken from the heart and tried my best, and yet all I could think was that I'd lost my notes and let people down.

But the reality was that The Stand was an amazing day. Deb's experience of the night could vouch for that. She often talks about how, on the night, she sat near the front and looked back across the crowds, totally overwhelmed. Just realizing how many people were 'with us' in our fight against this awful situation moved her to tears. As we stood on the stage to welcome everyone – Rob, Marion, Deb and myself – there was this massive eruption of cheering and applause. At the time this filled me with nerves, but Deb felt this lift, this incredible feeling of 'Oh, people are with us. We're not going to have to convince them. It's all right; they're with us.'

And they were. People were hungry to get involved and to do something. The organizations we had highlighted during the evening grew. People had been able to hear from their leaders and about all they'd been doing around the world. One charity said they'd never had so many people sign up as they did on that night! Children were sponsored to prevent them being exploited. People gave money. They joined campaigns. We had fifty to sixty organizations in the expo area. People were motivated. They were mobilized. They were given purpose. And people gave to us. They gave incredibly generously. We had 300 individuals committing to starting an Act for Justice group to help promote Hope for Justice and fundraise for us in their local areas. Finally, after months of dreaming, planning and panicking, the passion had met its purpose. A movement was born.

ANOTHER SIDE TO THE STORY
PATRICK THOMPSON, REND COLLECTIVE

I met Ben the year The Stand was happening. It was back in Northern Ireland and Ben and Debbie had been asked to help lead this youth weekend at my church. We clicked straight away, just chatting away about personal stuff. But then on the next day – the Sunday – Ben was speaking at the church. This was the first time I heard his heart for Hope for Justice. From then on I got loads of opportunities to hear of Ben's passion and vision for its work. Looking back, these initial times we hung out must have been right in the lead-up to The Stand, but you'd never have known that Ben was having severe financial difficulties or skipping meals and that sort of thing. I never knew that about him. And you'd never have been able to guess because he was just so excited about life in general! He was also incredibly driven towards the end goal he had in mind.

What Ben had spoken about at our church had great impact, but it was actually later, during the three years that followed our first meeting, that I was able to hear the details about Hope for Justice and the work they were involved in. We had spent a lot of time together since we had met, but this one occasion Ben invited me around to his in-laws' house in Northern Ireland to talk specifically about Hope for Justice. He told me the brutal, gritty truth about human trafficking. It was really hard to listen to. He then shared his vision for getting artists involved to help promote the cause. At the time, Rend Collective were at the start of our own journey and so weren't really playing a lot of shows. What he said had so much impact on me that I wanted to see something change, but I didn't really understand what my involvement would be. I played in a band that had sold fourteen records (to our family!).

For a long time, then, our involvement was merely a friendship. It was 2016 when we first began to partner Hope for Justice in a professional context. We were playing a UK tour in May, and I think for myself and the guys in the band it had always been a bit of a dream to support the work of Hope for Justice. At this point in Rend Collective's journey we had a reasonable degree of influence, and we wanted to use that influence to make a difference in other people's lives. And so when both Ben and the band were in Nashville we decided that Ben would come on our UK tour. It was a great opportunity for us to share the platform we have with something we really believe in. We love to make time in our gigs to talk about important causes like the one Hope for Justice fights for; we believe highlighting these kinds of issues is a huge part of worship.

Worship is what we are called to do with our entire lives. Our desire is that we wouldn't just gather people in a room to make them feel good, make them have a good time and make them dance and smile, though these are all great things! We want the worship to have a lasting impact, to be a practical thing that will be lived out beyond that night. Every night, what is really cool is that the benefit of the evening is not for the people who are sitting on seats in that room but for everyone outside the walls. We want to help mobilize people, as Ben does, to demonstrate the hope we have in practical ways.

The fact that we make time for organizations like Hope for Justice as part of our gigs is because we don't want people leaving thinking that worship is just what we do with our voices. And so each night after the first artist, I would get up and briefly introduce

Ben, and he would get up for about 18 minutes and knock it out of the park! But one of the sad things is that not everyone wants to hear about these issues. We received a reasonable amount of opposition. That is one of the reasons I respect Ben as much as I do. I hadn't really thought about it, but this is not an issue people enjoy hearing about. We probably got complaints every day saying it was an inappropriate thing to be talking about at that kind of gathering. This was really difficult to deal with because we feel we have a responsibility to the people who come to see us. Perhaps they were trying to shield their kids from this kind of thing and tell them in their own time. But at the same time it was so frustrating because we just felt like saying: 'This is a real issue and it is one we have to tackle. This is not an issue that we can just ignore and hope somebody else will sort it out. This is something that really has to be spoken about and hasn't been spoken about enough.'

So often it was difficult. I think Ben did a fantastic job; he didn't water it down but I don't think he ever went too far. It's not really going to change until people know about it, and that's what our hearts are set on, that's where Ben's heart lies, to make a difference. As a band we are definitely into supporting this, we are definitely into giving our time to help be a voice for this.

LOSING INTEGRITY DESTROYS CREDIBILITY.

Chapter six

MAGDALENE'S STORY

We arrived at the location where Magdalene was held. My colleague Emma led me into the room. I don't know if you've ever been to a developing country where you can see poverty everywhere, but there is another thing that hits me every time I step into a place of extreme poverty: that not only can you see it, you can smell it. It's difficult to describe but it's distinctive: the smell of exploitation. Though the family hadn't been there long, the smell was strong; it clung to my clothes.

When I walked into the room I saw a group of children, not far off my own children's age. Their backs were against the wall, their heads between their knees. It turned out they had been sitting this way for hours. The image of those 5-, 6-, 7-year-old children with their backs against the wall, surrounded by filth, in the middle of the day is now burned into my memory. They had been robbed of hope, they had been robbed of their dignity, their aspirations.

They were silent and nervous; I turned to Emma and said: 'Look, what can I do? I need to do something practical. What do you need me to do?' So she asked me to go and get them some food from the local supermarket. As I went round the aisles, I threw everything I could see in the trolley: clothing, food, supplies for the baby, the lot. Anything that could even begin to help meet their needs. I took it all back, but in the rush I'd forgotten to get something hot they could eat right away. Emma, responsible for coordinating this case, sent me out again. I and another colleague, Isaac, went out to get pizza. The wait for food seemed to take ages. I will never forget starting to feel hungry and then thinking what the children must be feeling.

When we finally got back I put all the food out on the table, fully anticipating that the children – who were still there with their heads between their knees – would run up and get the food. But they didn't. They didn't move. I turned to Emma and said: 'I don't understand! Why aren't they going to get the food?' She said: 'Ben, every night the trafficker would eat his dinner around the table, laughing and joking about his day all the while.' She pointed at them: 'These nine people would be sitting on the floor like animals, waiting for him to finish his meal. Then once he'd finished his meal, he would grab the scraps of food off the table and throw them on to the floor for the children to eat like animals.'

Suddenly I wasn't hungry any more. I had to leave the room for a while. I had tasted something in that moment. Do you know what it was? Perspective. Throughout the whole of our organizational journey I thought we'd had our own share of hardship, but I'd never had to sit on the floor; I've never had anyone throw scraps to me on the floor. These children were malnourished. And not just physically but emotionally and spiritually as well. That moment, that perspective, stayed with me.

Our team went to see them again after this rescue. The kids were running around, the baby had big chubby cheeks and the teenagers had baked the team a cake to say thank you for giving them back their freedom. Their mum once said to our team: 'If it wasn't for Hope for Justice, my children wouldn't have survived. My children wouldn't have survived!' No matter how hard it's been, it's moments like that, the moments in which you see hope, that keep you going. That was the moment that life changed for them, the moment they were no longer exploited, the moment they were free.

WHAT NOW?

I sat at my desk. The room felt simultaneously the size of an aircraft hangar and a broom cupboard. Cavernous and claustrophobic. Then the phone rang. I picked up:

'Hello, Hope for Justice. Ben Cooley speaking.' There was a slight pause.

'Wow. Did I call your direct line?' the voice asked.

'Kind of,' I replied. 'It's our only line.'

The dust had begun to settle following The Stand. All those sleepless nights wondering if anyone would attend; all those car journeys travelling from church to church sharing the vision of the event; all the coordinating of booking bands and speakers; all of the preparation – the blood, sweat and tears – was now over. It was over. The event had been a success; many organizations had benefited; children vulnerable to human trafficking had been sponsored. We had done it. But what next?

It was the Monday following the event, and I was sitting at a wobbly desk with just one phone for company. It was one of the loneliest moments I've ever experienced in Hope for Justice. For months and months I'd been surrounded by people, talking to the team every day. I'd been driven by appointments and decisions and tasks. I'd been running on adrenaline, people and caffeine for a long time. And now it was just me. Those people were no longer around me, those appointments no longer booked. And although the 'hard part' was seemingly over, those days were challenging. I was sitting there, trying to work out what on earth I would do going forward. The Stand had sparked passion and generated purpose, but what should I do with it now? How could I create something that harnessed the passion and purpose to help bring an end to modern-day slavery? How should I shape this? At that very moment we had 300 Act for Justice groups who were campaigning and fundraising locally all around the country and many more people giving to us. The event had put passion in people's hearts, but now we had to give them something practical to do with their hands. There were so many questions in my mind, but there was no-one to share them with. I was in an office, alone, with a really wobbly desk.

These days taught me that growth has to be incremental. I started in a basement and we had now moved to this small office. Change is not sustainable when it happens too quickly. It has to be measured. But although difficult, these days were also incredibly special. In many ways the founding principles of Hope for Justice were born during these days.

I've always known that integrity is one of the fundamental foundations of leadership. I saw it in my father and I've seen it watching other leaders I hugely respect. Losing integrity destroys credibility. When you hear of CEOs who cheat their companies out of money, or people who say they'll deliver something that they don't, it burns credibility. We had 300 people sign up to set up groups. I didn't want to lose integrity in their eyes. I wanted these amazing people to buy into the vision, to join us in the movement, to stick with us, be a part of the family. So I went silent on making any promises. I didn't start shooting my mouth off, saying 'We're going to the do this' and 'We're going to do that.'

I began working with Rob Allen and the board, wrestling with these big questions. There were people around me urging me to mobilize those who had signed up. But I went into slow mode. Why? Because I knew I had only one chance to start the movement and if I over-promised and under-delivered then we would lose everything. The Stand was merely an advertisement for a movement that was coming and a celebration of other organizations that were already established. But in those next few months, I really felt the importance of it. This year was pivotal to seeing our vision become a reality. In a letter to Lady Middleton, William Wilberforce wrote that he felt the importance of the abolition of the slave trade but also totally unequal to the task allotted him, though he wouldn't positively decline it. In 2009, I could totally relate to that. I saw the importance of the subject. I felt *completely* inadequate to the task allotted me but there was no way I would positively decline it. There I was, conscious of avoiding losing credibility and conscious of maintaining integrity.

In those days our vision centred on India. The experience I had in that country never left me. We knew we could support the work out there. And that was what was driving us. I wrote a proposal for our trustees suggesting that we could become a conduit for the organization working against trafficking in India. I did the presentation. I shared the vision.

And the trustees said no.

I was utterly devastated. I couldn't believe it. But you see, here is the interesting thing: they saw greater potential than I had. I'd presented basement thinking; their vision was arena-sized.

They pushed me forward. I've surrounded myself with people who aren't 'yes' people. That has been one of my greatest assets. They're people who are with me, who are for me, but they're always willing to raise the bar, to expand the vision and challenge safe thinking. And that was the moment when they said they thought we needed to do something in the UK: we needed to do something about Emma's story and the countless others like her.

My initial reaction was that I didn't want to do it. I wanted the easier path, the safer option. But deep down, in the core of my being, I knew there was something right about this. This was the vision that would shape the movement. This is my country. This is where I was born. These are my people. The passion began to grow, not just for the issue but for the nation. I wanted to see an end to human trafficking in the UK. Within the board there were lots of opinions about how we would approach this. Some were for aftercare, some for advocacy. While I knew they were right in focusing on the UK, I also knew that rescue was the right vision for Hope for Justice in that season. We couldn't do everything, but we could do something. We got external help to assist us in adjusting that vision so that everyone was on the same page. It is a difficult balance as the CEO of a charitable organization, going with the vision you feel is right and submitting this to your board and allowing them meaningful input. If you're a young leader reading this and you struggle with submission, you may think you have all the right answers. Let me tell you: you don't. I certainly didn't. One of the best and most important characteristics of a leader – of any age, but particularly young leaders – is teachability and humility.

Persuading our board to believe in this common goal was not achieved by force. It was through listening to them and hearing what their passions were and then proceeding with an attitude of humility. You sometimes need a fighter. Winston Churchill was the right leader during the Second World War but not for the peace that followed. Only a few months after the war ended, he was replaced by Clement Attlee. What I learned in those days was that I couldn't just fight, like I'd fought with sheer passion to make The Stand a success. I needed a different Ben Cooley to sit in that boardroom. I needed to be smarter, more refined. I needed to hone my communication skills. I needed to share reasoned arguments for what the outcomes would be and why we were best placed to achieve that, to remain teachable and humble.

The defining moment came when I introduced our trustees to 'Slavery Boulevard'. Imagine it costs £100,000 to build a house and we have enough land to build six houses, but we only have £100,000. If each house costs £100,000 to build, do I start six houses or do I complete one house? Once that first house is built, it can then generate income to build the second. Once the second is built, we do the same to build the third, and so on. Imagine this is Slavery Boulevard. The first house is prevention, the second house is rescue, the third house is advocacy and prosecution, the fourth house is aftercare, the fifth house is second-phase aftercare and the sixth house is political lobbying and the national infrastructure.

I presented this to the board. I told them we only had enough money to build one house, so which house did we want to build? If we try to build all six from the start, we would quickly drain resources, run out of cash and end up with six partly built houses. So which one do we want to do? We had already started rescuing victims in a small way. We had employed our first team member focusing on rescues and he was already seeing results. It strengthened my argument to the board because we already had a track record. It wasn't much but there were results. Maybe if we put more results behind this and built a team, we really could see some significant impact. It was unique. No-one else was doing it. We came to a unified and focused vision. We would rescue victims of modern-day slavery in the United Kingdom.

★ ★ ★

With a shared direction in mind, our team grew. The tiny office we had started in was simply no longer big enough. So one of our team generously lent his garage for his staff to work from. Glamorous, right?

But being in two locations made it difficult to sustain a united culture. Even so, I understood that you can be in the same room as someone and not be united. For example, I can be in the living room with my kids and not really 'with them', perhaps because I'm on my phone, doing emails or my mind is just somewhere else. I am not present. Proximity does not equate to unity. It was then that I came to a difficult realization: I didn't like our organization.

Even within the same building there was division between us. Some people could no longer see where they fitted into the vision of the organization because we hadn't built the right kind of culture. I discovered then that you either set the culture or the culture sets you. I'd focused so much on the vision that I forgot about the culture. Why you do something is hugely important, but how you do it is just as important. I'd given so much attention to what we did and why we did it, that the how we did it had got lost. Clearly, something had to change.

That's when we started a new tradition. Every time we achieved a rescue, we would crack open a bottle of champagne.

On that bottle we would write the victim's name, reinforcing the vision. Rescue is what we do and we do it together. Every single rescue, every single member of the team would gather together and we would celebrate. Whether you were a receptionist, a lawyer, an aftercare specialist or the CEO, you knew that what you were doing was making a difference. It was a tradition that grew. We would share on social media that we were celebrating another rescue and we would receive messages from all over the country from our various Act for Justice groups, who shared photos of themselves cracking open their own bottles of champagne. We celebrated together. We would see an end to this together.

With a culture of togetherness and celebration driving us forward, I knew Hope for Justice didn't just need people with great credentials, it needed people with great character. This is not easy. I must have interviewed hundreds of people over the past few years, but that process is not suited to identifying character. Character is proved over time, through hardship and good fortune. Take Emma, the coordinator in Magdalene's story. Emma is the only person I've ever interviewed three times and, perhaps naturally, by the time of her third interview she was actually relatively scared of me. And so when she began working for us, whenever we were in a meeting together she would be quite timid. But not on the day we rescued Magdalene and her family. Faced with this challenge, faced with this injustice, Emma owned her leadership capacity in a way I couldn't have imagined. It was amazing to see this strong, dynamic woman leading this family into freedom.

It was also during this season that I met Jeremy. Jeremy was a Borough Commander in Hertfordshire Constabulary. I had connected with Jeremy through one of our trustees. We met for lunch and, as we talked, I could tell that he was a man of great substance and experience. He had been there, done it and got the t-shirt. But there was something more impressive: his character.

His character was completely different from mine, but it was complementary. I was restless. When we rescued one victim, I wanted the second. When we rescued two people, I wanted the third. I was completely motivated to *do* something. Jeremy also wanted to do something, but he wanted to do it *right*. He wanted to do it methodically and sustainably. I would normally have worked at full pelt, all systems go, all the time. Jeremy introduced a new gear to my life. When we discussed life, when we discussed the organization, when we discussed the vision, he would always come back to: 'So how will we make this work?' I would want to be innovative and pioneering but Jeremy introduced policies and infrastructure. He would emphasize sustainable approaches. He didn't want relationships for the short term but relationships for the long term.

In these discussions and during this time, I felt as though I was growing up. I learned what it meant to build an organization and a movement that would last. There were moments when the restless got frustrated with the reliable. There were moments I wanted to go faster and further. But in Jeremy I had someone who would suggest the right pace of growth. It trained me, and I've since gathered lots of people who can provide this input. I've realized that I am the by-product of the environment I have deliberately placed myself in. That's why I've surrounded myself with people who are better than me. I can't do it all, so I want the best people around me to do it with me.

ANOTHER SIDE TO THE STORY
JEREMY ALFORD, FORMER HOPE FOR JUSTICE
DIRECTOR OF OPERATIONS

Out of the blue a retired pastor friend of mine rang me up. We'd not seen each other or spoken for several months. He said he'd been to an 'event' and heard a young guy called Ben Cooley speak with great conviction about an organization called Hope for Justice. Because of the type of work I did, he thought I'd find it interesting to get in touch to find out more. Looking back on it, this phone call was about to change the next chapter of my life significantly, but neither of us realized it at the time.

I'd retired from the police service a year earlier. The past five years of my service were spent as a Chief Superintendent, a role I had found hugely fulfilling as a Borough Commander in the west of Hertfordshire. I'd spent the previous five years as the senior detective in the Hertfordshire Constabulary. I was working for the Mayor of London as part of a team developing a strategy for dealing with violence against women and girls. I was content. I wasn't looking for a job. But that didn't mean I wasn't about to be led into one.

Out of no more than a mild curiosity and, if I am honest, a sense of duty towards Tony, my old pastor mate, I picked up the phone one day and rang Hope for Justice. The phone was answered by Rob White, the Chair of Trustees. Rob was not someone who would usually be in the office to answer the phone! The fact that he was there at that time was uncanny. I explained who I was and apologized for potentially wasting his time. What he told me next hit me like a hammer. It was clear I needed to know more. It just so happened that Hope for Justice were looking for someone with relatively senior policing experience to review the work of their investigative team.

Little did I know that first day when I boarded the train bound for Manchester what I was letting myself in for! I met Ben Cooley. I was confronted with a young man who was extraordinarily passionate about his vision to bring an end to human slavery. He was so honest. He had made mistakes along the way (haven't we all?), and he wanted some help and advice.

To cut a long story short, I left Manchester convinced that I could take a look at the way Hope for Justice did things and could help in some small way. I carried out the review and recommended some new ways of operating. I presented it to the board of trustees and got offered a job! I hadn't gone for one, but I am so thankful that I was handed the opportunity to make a difference in my own small way.

Ben is right. We were (are) very different people. I honestly don't recognize the Jeremy Ben so graciously describes in this chapter. I am humbled by his description of my character and that he has learnt from me. Well, if he has learnt from me, I learned so many lessons from him. I learned the importance of passionately believing in what you do, of having a vision and of striving endlessly to bring that vision about. With no hint of false modesty, I do not consider myself to be inspirational. Ben is inspirational; he also has a wicked sense of humour and a terrible American accent that he puts on at every opportunity! He is loud, he is self-confident and brings people along with him for the ride. He is an up-front guy. I am more of a behind-the-scenes type of bloke!

It was my job to start building the infrastructure, writing the policies and procedures and taking things one step at a time to help build trust with police forces and to present Hope for Justice as what it is now: a professional organization that knows what it is doing and does it right.

I know I frustrated Ben. Policies are not the most exciting things in the world. They are not achieved overnight. They take time. I had to be boring! For every visionary there has to be at least one pragmatist. We had difficult conversations. I often failed to grasp Ben's vision for a particular aspect of the work, be it legal, aftercare or other areas of operation that I controlled as Director of Operations. On an almost daily basis he would come into the office and spend time on his latest idea for doing things differently. I got through it by saying 'Good idea. Let me think about it and we'll talk tomorrow.' That way we managed to capture the brilliant ideas, of which there were many, and jettison the outlandish, of which there were also a few!

In the two and a bit years I spent at the heart of Hope for Justice, with the help of Ben and some great professional people around me I think we started to gain some real momentum and build genuine trust with various agencies, including law enforcement. There is never a good time to leave an organization, but I came to see that my work, although not complete, was well underway and could be accomplished by others.

I always keep a close eye on Hope for Justice and its continuing work. It is amazing, groundbreaking, earth-shattering and all the other superlatives you can think of. Hope for Justice, its work and all those trafficked people out there still to be rescued, are always in my prayers.

**FOR HE
WILL DELIVER
THE NEEDY
WHO CRY OUT.**

Chapter seven

LUCAS'S STORY

Lucas was homeless in his home country. He had no-one to turn to for help and was struggling to find work. The weather was extremely cold and he was desperate. He was at a homeless shelter one day, where some people were recruiting people to work in the UK. They were targeting those who didn't speak English and hadn't been to the UK before; they said they had found success in the UK and were returning to find more people. They said he would be well paid and would be provided with accommodation and food.

With few other options, Lucas chose to take the risk and go with them. He arrived at a house where that night he had to share a mattress with two other men. He thought this might just be a one-off, that things would improve, but sadly that wasn't the case.

He was put to work in a bed factory, doing hard physical labour for eleven hours a day. After two weeks he had earned £10. The people running the factory gave the money straight to the traffickers. Most of the time Lucas was having to sleep on the floor in an overcrowded house where up to forty men were living at a time, where he and his fellow workers were not allowed in the kitchen and only permitted to use the shower once a week. If

Lucas didn't do what the traffickers told him he would not be given any food. He had no money, spoke no English and didn't know the area in which he was living, so had no way to ask for help. He was trapped.

By the time Hope for Justice found Lucas, he had lost a lot of weight and was desperate and frightened. However, after spending some time in a safe house, he felt able to report to the police what happened and help bring the perpetrators to justice.

STRUCTURE, STRATEGY, SUSTAINABILITY

As Hope for Justice continued to grow, so did I. I was learning every day, from the people around me and the experiences we had shared.

At the beginning of our journey I had spoken of the vision I had to organize a big event. I was now learning that that was entirely the wrong message. An event is not a vision. The true vision behind The Stand was to mobilize people and find the resources that would allow us to employ others to rescue victims, advocate on their behalf and provide aftercare, and, ultimately, to be able to offer the same freedom to every single slave.

One thing that saddens me about our generation today is that we are often distracted by stuff I would call 'non-visions'. Hoping for a suitable building to house a cause, for example, is not a vision. A building is a facility. It is a vehicle for a vision. Our vision is about transforming elements of society, about seeing every business operating in a manner that pays its staff fairly, that sees its responsibility to society and not just the profit margin. Our vision is that we see governments putting policies in place that protect the most vulnerable. That is the vision, and we must hold fast to it in the face of many other distracting non-visions.

In this new era of expansion I became even more aware that there were certain skill bases that I was missing. Organizing The Stand, I had been too busy to self-assess or compare what we were doing to what others were doing. But now I began to analyse, and in some senses over-analyse. I'd begun to realize what I was and what I was not. So in order to educate and develop myself, I deliberately built relationships with those who could help me.

You should know that I often feel intimidated when surrounded by our team. We have people working for us now who have managed thousands of staff. We have people working for us who have held extremely senior positions within some of the largest police forces in the country. Every time our organization has gone through a season of growth, I have experienced something like an identity crisis. Every time we have become bigger, I've had to ask myself: 'Where do I fit in this vision, in this organization?' I've heard some people say: 'I am not defined by what I do, rather by who I am.' But who I am is intrinsically linked with what I do, and I'd *love* to say I'm totally secure, that my identity is not tied to Hope for Justice, but this is all I know. This is who I am. And particularly in this new season, I tried to learn and in some senses *had* to learn to be all right with being scared. I had to learn to be all right with not knowing for periods who I was or who I was turning into. I may often feel intimidated, but the vision is too important for me to be insecure and, because of that insecurity, not to involve the very experienced people in the Hope for Justice team. I need their wisdom with structure and strategy.

I remember getting in touch with this chap called Peter Elson. He'd been introduced through a mutual friend and he ran a large company in the UK. I needed someone like Peter to answer questions such as: 'How do you structure your team?' 'How about your meetings?' 'What does organizational infrastructure look like?' 'What level of accountability do you have with your key team?' Just like in Mumbai, the list of questions went on and on.

I mentioned earlier that Jeremy Alford and I were very different people. Peter and I were *totally* different. Peter's the kind of guy who will spend hours and hours considering a single question or issue, and in the early days of meeting with Peter I would keep trying to steer him away from certain questions and he would keep coming back to them. I was quickly learning the importance of surrounding myself with people who think differently from me. Thanks to them, I'm a different Ben Cooley from the one who picked up the phone and booked the NEC Arena. It's not that I've lost my audacity; it's certainly not that I've lost my passion. But they've strengthened me, helped me mature. I'm now more deliberate, less knee-jerk, more, well, boring (just kidding!).

★ ★ ★

Through this team effort we were building something sustainable. We were rescuing victims. We were seeing our organization's objectives become a reality. We were seeing people transformed from just surviving in life to thriving. But we were also noticing something.

In one area where we had rescued a number of victims, there was a worrying trend. Some 61% of victims we were rescuing had gone to various agencies before they were rescued by Hope for Justice, but had not been identified as victims of human trafficking. I couldn't comprehend how this might be possible. Things are now very different and the story is improving but, back then, we knew these agencies had a lot of different priorities, of which trafficking was only one. They can't know everything, and they certainly didn't have the resources to cover all areas. However, when vulnerable victims of crime were being turned away when they asked for help, something needed to change.

We had a small team. Our reach was wide but not deep. We'd rescued victims in many parts of the country but had no deep impact in any particular region. We were stretched. So as a team we started talking: what if we could make a serious impact in this region where 61% of victims were being turned away?

We decided we would send a new team into that region and own responsibility for the area. This team became our first investigative hub. We took on six hugely experienced former police officers, who would proactively identify victims of human trafficking and rescue them from exploitation. This region had the fourth-largest police force in the UK but one of the lowest numbers of identified victims of human trafficking. We would work in partnership with local police forces and other agencies to develop cases and go upstream to identify the perpetrators. This was our first regional office, but we didn't want it to be known as 'Hope for Justice North East' or 'Office Number Two'. That just wasn't us. So we decided to name the office after the first victim we ever rescued. We called the office 'Emma's Hub'.

In its first year, Emma's Hub assisted and rescued 110 victims of human trafficking. It was incredible. The youngest victim rescued that year was just 1 year old; the eldest was 59. We saw victims from all categories of slavery, but predominantly we found those trapped in forced labour. There were victims who were held in tiny basements for five years. We saw people whose hands had been crippled because they had been forced to dig holes in the frost and freezing temperatures of winter without any tools. They broke their fingers but were refused medical attention by their traffickers. We found victims caught in domestic servitude. One was 19 years old, forced to sleep next to a toilet.

In this year we were also able to begin to tackle a case where victims were being forced to make beds for some of the largest high-street shopping brands. Lucas's story was one of many similar, and the same names and places started to crop up over and over again. We recognized links between these cases and realized this was much bigger than just the odd instance of forced labour. This was an organized trafficking gang.

Victims can sometimes be reluctant to speak to the police at first, but after some time spent in a safe, stable place they will often be much more willing to report the crime. As we built up a picture of what was going on, we shared as much intelligence as we could with the police and encouraged victims to submit any information they had so they could build a case against the perpetrators. We also worked with other safe houses and organizations to support the victims through the process. It worked. First the traffickers doing the recruiting were arrested, and then eventually the factory owner was prosecuted for human trafficking and was described in the press as employing a 'slave workforce'. This was the first case of its kind in the UK, and was a big victory both for us and all our partners on the case.

We were making a massive difference and, importantly, were building a picture of what human trafficking looked like in the UK. We were identifying victims and where they were coming from, and in doing so were discovering where the gaps were in the system. And we were able to take this to the regional Police and Crime Commissioner, who was passionate about making a difference to those most vulnerable in society. We humbly suggested three ways in which we could help. First, we could train local police officers in how to spot the signs of human trafficking. Second, we could help set up a multi-agency working group that would be able to identify the gaps in that region. Third, we would work in conjunction with their police force on every investigation.

The Police and Crime Commissioner agreed, and because of this partnership not only were we able to continue rescuing victims in conjunction with the police, we were also able to train 3,800 frontline agency workers, including police officers, NGOs, social services and others. As we identified some of the gaps in protection, we were given permission to work on effective strategies to plug those gaps. Two years later that region saw a 190% increase in the numbers of victims of slavery being identified and had the highest number of identified victims in the country. Emma's Hub had taken all of our passion and provided it with a structure. A structure that was working.

There were many reasons Emma's Hub had such an impact then, and still does today. One of the central reasons was that we were not working alone. Emma's Hub provides an open and collaborative structure in which many organizations and individuals are empowered to play their part. The end of slavery cannot become a reality through the efforts of Hope for Justice alone nor will it come from those of any other single charity or agency. Emma's Hub taught me just how powerful effective partnerships can be. Great strategies are important, but if the systems and people implementing that strategy cannot work together or, worse still, cannot be trusted, the strategy is destined to fail.

Aid strategy is important, but arguably not as important as structural reform. How do we bring rule of law? How do we combat corruption? How do we encourage a just society? How do we see fairness and equality become reality? How do we make sure the law enforcement officers in Uganda are protecting the widow whose land has just been taken from her? How do we ensure that when a girl in India is raped, the police are not a part of the problem but rather a part of the solution?

In the Western world corruption may not be as prevalent as in the developing world, but human trafficking is a crime that calls for us to adapt our policies, our strategies and our practices in order to combat it effectively. I don't think that Western governments are knowingly complicit in the crime of modern-day slavery, but I could name businesses that are perceived to be ethical and are highly recognizable but have victims in their supply chains. It may not come as a surprise to you, but many of the clothes we buy, the furniture we have in our homes and the foods we eat on a daily basis use slavery at some point in their supply chains. The desire to change individual lives is still very much at the heart of our movement. But to end slavery one person at a time, we cannot be blind to the need for structural transformation to see that vision become a reality. And if there is anything we did right in this season, it was not just to rescue victims, to equip other agencies to identify victims and to assist in prosecutions, but more than that it was to look at the core systemic problems and seek to address them. And that is what we did.

It's also important that we give credit where it's due and recognize the significant role government has played in supporting the fight against modern-day slavery. Particular honour must go to Theresa May, the former Home Secretary of the UK who then became Prime Minister. Through her work on the Modern Slavery Act 2015, the legislation in the UK is as strong as it has ever been on human trafficking and provides a robust framework for the rescue and restoration of victims and the prosecution of traffickers.

The region in which we based Emma's Hub became the area with the highest number of identified victims of human trafficking in the country. There has been a monumental change in how victims are being identified.

Emma's Hub gave us a framework and model that could be replicated in other environments. It also showed us that this was not just a momentary change, it was a sustainable change. There are two key components: sustainability and replicability. That's how we will see real change not just within the lives of individuals but throughout businesses, governments and ultimately society.

ANOTHER SIDE TO THE STORY
PHILIPPA ROBERTS, SOLICITOR AND LEGAL DIRECTOR,
HOPE FOR JUSTICE

I have always had a passion for justice. Indeed, my decision to train as a lawyer was fuelled by my desire to use the skills and knowledge I would acquire to fight injustice.

I first learned about Hope for Justice when I was working for International Justice Mission in India. I met Ben after being asked to be on the steering group for the first event run by Hope for Justice, The Stand. As part of that group, I was exposed to the work of Hope for Justice and became really inspired by Ben and an organization with such an ambitious vision. Some time after The Stand, I met up with Ben in a coffee shop and discussed how we were going to change the world! That's where it all started; I began doing some volunteer work at Hope for Justice and then became a full-time member of staff a couple of years later.

Although Hope for Justice operates on a global scale, the advances made in policy and legislation in the UK over the past few years are important to note. This is because they can operate as a reference point for other countries in the global effort to combat modern slavery.

Wider European legislation has largely provided the framework for the law on modern slavery in the UK. The Council of Europe Convention on Action against Trafficking in Human Beings and, subsequently, European Directive 2011/36/EU set out obligations regarding what governments and states should be doing to prevent human trafficking, prosecute perpetrators and protect victims. In the UK, the State is required to create a system for identifying victims, define criminal offences and provide support for victims. It was in response to the European framework that the UK developed the National Referral Mechanism (NRM), which provides a system for identifying victims and ensuring that they receive holistic support to meet their basic needs for safety and stability. Such support includes securing safe accommodation, help in accessing mental health services, assistance finding employment and support in understanding their legal rights.

Soon after Theresa May became Home Secretary, she grew very passionate about the issue of modern-day slavery and created the impetus for significant change in the UK's approach to the problem. With this new focus, Parliament passed the Modern Slavery Act 2015, which consolidated the criminal offences associated with trafficking and slavery into one piece of legislation, and aimed to increase prosecution rates, make the UK a hostile environment for traffickers and give guidance on how victims are identified and protected. The Act's significance is far-reaching: not only was it the first major piece of domestic legislation on slavery for well over a hundred years but it also helped to raise awareness of modern-day slavery as a contemporary issue in the UK among politicians and the public.

Five or six years ago, the general consensus on the phenomenon of modern slavery was that it was exclusive to the Global South – something that no longer occurred in the West. There is now an increased realization, however, that slavery is a problem on our doorsteps. The Modern Slavery Act is not perfect but it is the start of what is needed. We are seeing more of the estimated 13,000 victims identified in the UK; we're observing greater collaborative work between police forces and statutory and non-statutory agencies – efforts that are absolutely vital for effectively combating modern slavery. Furthermore, consolidating the legislation has placed the UK at the forefront of international responses to slavery. The Act includes revolutionary steps – such as the creation of an Independent Anti-Slavery Commissioner and the introduction of specific measures to tackle slavery in supply chains.

Yet just as important as increasing prosecutions and creating more hostile environments for traffickers is the need to ensure that, when identified, victims receive support to recover from their experiences – to help them not only survive but thrive in life. In addition, support helps to prevent victims from being exploited or trafficked again. The everyday work of Hope for Justice's advocacy team reveals that many mainstream services, such as those for housing and welfare, fail to meet adequately the specific and often complex needs of modern slavery victims. Without staunch and sustained advocacy, the victims are too often left vulnerable and, in some cases, destitute. Invariably, a lack of support has an impact on the ability of those rescued to make informed choices, such as whether to cooperate with a police investigation and/or pursue civil compensation.

The link between the support and legal aspects is essential. Many victims do want to cooperate with criminal investigations – not simply for their own sakes but also to ensure that others are not subjected to similar experiences. When victims receive the support they need, they are in a much better position to give the best evidence in court. Those who have been trafficked and enslaved need to feel safe, supported and protected when they come forward to cooperate with criminal investigations; making sure they feel secure as witnesses strengthens the likelihood of successful prosecutions. Even if victims choose not to work with the police, their information is crucial to intelligence gathering on wider criminal networks and how best to disrupt them. It can also lead to the rescue of other people.

Like many other non-governmental organizations (NGOs), Hope for Justice is active on the ground. As experienced practitioners in this field, we have developed extensive knowledge that enables us to work with governments and other relevant agencies for the benefit of all those caught up in trafficking and slavery. Working together, we not only facilitate the rescue and restoration of individual victims and fight for justice across the globe but we also contribute to the goal of ending modern-day slavery for good.

HE WILL RESCUE
THEM FROM
OPPRESSION
AND VIOLENCE.

Chapter eight

ZOE'S STORY

The week before Christmas we received an extremely worrying report about a young Eastern European woman, Zoe, a suspected victim of human trafficking. She was being forced to work as a prostitute on the south coast of England. The information we received was so detailed we knew we had a window of opportunity, but only if we acted fast. Over the next few hours, we checked our facts and became increasingly concerned. It was clear that she was part of a trafficking ring run by a number of incredibly dangerous criminals.

Zoe's life wasn't in danger, but she was being controlled. When we did investigate, Zoe gave us the indication that she didn't want the police involved; she would bolt and run if the police approached her at all. Zoe had come from an area in Eastern Europe that had a long history of poverty and mistrust of authority, and she had wanted to escape to a better life. She was incredibly vulnerable. That's where the exploitation comes in.

I'm often asked how people end up being trafficked. It's always because they are vulnerable in some way, whether it's to do with economic reasons, mental health issues or lack of education.

There are also several vulnerable population groups. Look at the Roma community, for example, one of the most exploited peoples in the world. They are vulnerable often because they are isolated. Zoe herself was incredibly isolated, with a mistrust of law enforcement. We often meet victims who don't want to engage with any form of authority, and are more likely to trust people who come from a charity or the well-meaning public.

So we met Zoe and started building a rapport. In that time we were trying to create an environment in which she felt safe and secure enough, and trusted us enough, that she would be able to leave the exploitation and move into aftercare. In the weeks it took to do this, she was moved. We were devastated. We believed she was sold on. Our team spent weeks trying to find her and eventually they did, by tracking down her picture on a website advertising her services. The profile was different, with a different name, but we knew it was her. The team made arrangements to meet her, but she wasn't expecting to see us. The moment she recognized one of our team, she was completely gripped by fear. She didn't know if we were good or bad, if we were responsible for her being sold again, but she had no-one else to trust, so she decided to trust us.

Petrified, she got in the car. One of our team described to me how disturbed Zoe was. She was frantic. When we arrived in the aftercare facility, Zoe started to see that this might actually be genuine, that we were telling the truth. She turned to our team member and said: 'It's real isn't it? Tonight I'm not gonna get exploited? I'm not gonna get abused?' He turned to her and said, 'Yeah, it's real Zoe.' Just then Zoe burst into floods of tears.

He said to her: 'You know what, Zoe? You're a princess. You're a daughter of the King.' Zoe was sobbing and sobbing and he heard her whisper: 'I'm a princess. I'm a princess.' Not long after that Zoe gave us some intelligence that led to a police raid, and other people were identified as victims of modern slavery.

Slavery is about the grading of human beings; it stems from the mentality that there are people and races who are worth less than others. And when people are trafficked they start believing this lie about themselves, that they are worth less, that they are worthless. One man we helped described the moment when he stood in front of two people haggling over his price; his trafficker was asking for £300 and the other guy insisted that he wasn't worth that much. Every human being wants to be valued and cherished, and if we can make that breakthrough and convince someone of it, it's a powerful moment.

ZOE'S CHALLENGE

What we had built was working. Emma's Hub was doing what we intended it to do. We were seeing rescues. But we knew we needed to do more. Our supporters and Abolition Groups (formerly Act for Justice Groups) had seen the impact we were making in the North East, but they wanted to see the same changes in their own regions. The desire for action was growing.

I'll never forget the moment when we were ready to announce the launch of our second hub during our annual Hope Conference. The growing demand for hubs saw the level of anticipation soar higher and higher among our supporters as they stood wondering whether this next one might be in their area. It was incredibly humbling to witness an excitement so huge, to see such passion among our supporters for the work we were doing. I remember standing there on this platform. I was just about to announce the location of 'Zoe's Hub'. I could see people leaning in expectantly. I remember seeing one particular group who started holding hands in anticipation of what I was about to say: it was in their region that we'd decided to open Zoe's Hub.

I'll never forget the delight on their faces. We launched Zoe's Hub in response to a demand, because this movement had momentum. Announcing this expansion made it clear to everyone in the room that the fight against modern-day slavery was now in full motion. It was a wonderful moment. But the big difference between this moment and the launch of Emma's Hub was that we now knew the cost. Zoe's Hub was a leap for us financially. We knew the risk, but the risk of not doing it was far greater, so we needed funding. As the groups around the room celebrated, they knew that the money would need to be found somewhere, somehow. But we already had a plan, one we were about to share.

In the weeks preceding telling people about the new hub, I had one of my friends round at my house. Tom was an actor in a UK-based television soap opera. He had played the same role for ten years and built a pretty high profile. We were discussing how we would raise the money for the new hub. We knew it would cost a lot of money: £263,500 to be precise. Racking our brains for ideas, Tom suggested we do a run. 'That's a stupid idea!' I thought, 'I mean, who likes to run?' Well, in reality, there are a lot of people who like to run, but I'm not one of them. Stupid idea, Tom. Vetoed. Next! We spoke about other types of challenge. My leaning was heavily towards eating challenges, but apparently people don't give much money to that! Finally we came up with the answer. We'd do a cycle ride. I'd ridden a bicycle before, so I thought: 'Yeah, I can cycle. How hard can it be?' But we didn't want to do any old cycle route. We wanted it to mean something. We wanted it to have a story.

We had recently rescued Zoe. She had been trafficked from Latvia to Southampton. And so having decided we were going to do a bike ride to fund Zoe's Hub, we thought what better route than to follow her journey? This part, at least, we agreed was a great idea. I phoned my mate Gareth to tell him. He was quieter than usual, almost stunned in disbelief. And he wasn't the only one. With the vision of our journey crystallizing in my head, I started telling more and more people: 'We're going to do it, we're going to cycle from Latvia to Southampton.'

Now let me just take a moment at this point to offer a word of advice. If you're ever planning on doing any long-distance journey or challenge, I would strongly recommend utilizing the power of online maps before you tell everyone what you're going to be doing. The reason is that at this point in our fundraising plan, without looking at online maps and without any expertise to inform me otherwise, I thought Latvia was next to France! Sadly (for me!), this was not the case. In fact Latvia is nowhere near France; it actually shares a border with Russia which, it turns out, is quite far away: 2,715 kilometres far away to be specific. And we were talking about 2,715 kilometres in 19 days – longer than the Tour de France – to be even more *painfully* specific.

But it was too late. After we'd decided on cycling along the route of Zoe's journey, we flew over to Latvia to do a recce. We wanted to see how feasible it was. Sensible, right? But sitting on the plane, we saw a first-hand reminder of why we were thinking of doing this. Right behind us was a young girl, sandwiched between two big guys. She had no luggage with her whatsoever. When we got to the airport terminal she was bundled into the back of a car and driven off. We didn't know for sure that she was being trafficked, but it seemed likely; it reminded us why we were about to take on something epic to try and combat this crime. With this image fresh in my mind, we began to film a promotional trailer for the challenge. 'We're going to do a bike ride from Latvia to Southampton in two weeks.' The words spilled out of my mouth. Tom looked on in surprise. After we'd finished filming he said: 'You do realize you've just told everybody we're going to cycle this in two weeks? And it's two thousand miles?!' Just like with The Stand, it seemed we had jumped in two feet first and then had to think logistically about how we were going to pull this thing off, broadcasting what our vision was and then figuring out how to make it a reality.

But the vision of our bike ride was becoming a reality, one we shared at the Hope Conference. Shortly after announcing the launch of Zoe's Hub, I also explained how we were going to raise the money to fund it. Zoe's Hub would be funded by Zoe's Challenge, and we invited others to join us. If I was going to cycle from Latvia to Southampton, maybe some other people would want to come as well. Well, we discovered that day that our supporters are actually quite sensible. None of them, apart from two other people, wanted to cycle the length and breadth of Europe. Go figure.

Perhaps it was because Zoe's Challenge was actually bigger than I thought, but the build-up to it actually went really well. In many ways it had come at the optimum time. Tom was just about to leave the soap opera he'd been playing in, with his character going out in a live episode broadcast to over ten million people. The media were interested in interviewing him about his time on the show, inviting him on to all kinds of breakfast and daytime programmes. We knew that each of them would ask him the same question: 'What's next?' It was a brilliant opportunity for him to say: 'Well actually, what I'm going to do is cycle from Latvia to Southampton following the journey of a girl called Zoe.' Suddenly we could use this amazing platform to share the story of Zoe, the story of Hope for Justice and the issue of human trafficking. We were able to get our voice out to millions and millions of people. We were able to get a significant online following of people tracking our journey. It was really special. But then the day came. We landed in Latvia.

I remember the night before the challenge began. We were in Riga. Riga is an amazing city; it's so beautiful. We were staying in a nice hotel, had had some great food, and for a brief moment I'd started to think it would be quite a nice holiday if it was like this the whole time! But the sinister side of the city was impossible to ignore. The sex industry is rife, and in the evening people, ride around on rickshaws trying to get you into clubs to see girls. This was yet another reminder of why we were doing this. As I went to bed the night before the challenge, I couldn't sleep. I'd like to say it was because of the excitement, but I wasn't excited. I'd come to the realization that we'd been on a flight that day that had taken hours. I was now about to begin to cycle back. There was no return ticket here. We were cycling back.

Isaac Stott was our cameraman for the trip and he was the life and soul of the party. Little did we know just how much we would need his enthusiasm in the coming days. Isaac is an incredible guy. He oversees much of the creative media output from Hope for Justice and is one of the most talented designers I've ever met. He's also hysterical. Fuelled by his enthusiasm and our passion for change, we cycled the whole of Latvia on that first day. Day one done, and it had gone well. I was feeling pretty positive: I'd just cycled through an entire country in a day. I was feeling good!

Next came day two. As we cycled through Lithuania, the positivity waned a little but we carried on, one pedal-stroke at a time. Pedal, pedal, pedal: the monotony of the exercise was starting to get boring. But then we saw something that shocked me to the core. I watched on as I saw a car run into a little kid on his bike, right in front of my eyes. The child was lying on the road; the car stopped, the driver got out, picked him up and put him at the side of the road. Then he drove off. Some passers-by ran to help the child; it looked as if he'd broken his leg. We stood on the other side of a busy road and quickly realized there was little we could do to help. So, shaken and confused, we had to ride on, with a very clear reminder of just how dangerous this country could be.

Then we got to Poland. Now, with my new-found discovery of online maps, I knew that Poland was massive. It's huge. But nothing could prepare me for the reality of it. And I'm sure there are beautiful parts of Poland, but the route we had decided to take was just tree after tree after tree. Pedal, tree, pedal, tree, pedal, tree. To keep things fun we started doing awards for each other at the end of the day: who's the slowest (I got that); the most unfit (me again!)? But even with our own evening award ceremonies to look forward to, nothing could have prepared us for the boredom. This country was never ending. As we continued cycling, I felt robbed of my initial passion. Lost in the monotony of it all, there was a moment when I hit new levels of boredom. 'I can't be bothered', I thought.

Then I looked down. And there it was: all the motivation I could want to get me going again. There was a wild wolf. A *wild . . . wolf!* Running next to me. Dribbling! Suddenly I seemed to find energy. I loved cycling again! In that moment of boredom and tiredness, I now had a dual motivation: the end of modern-day slavery and personal survival. Pressing on, pedalling on, we got through Poland.

Then we hit Germany. Well into the throes of the challenge, this is where things started to change. Something was reinforced for me in Germany, and the gravity of that lesson was undeniable: the danger with implementing any vision is not at the start or the end; it is right in the middle of the journey. Starting something can be easy. At the start you've got nothing to lose: you've got passion, you've got energy and you have everything to gain. Nor is the danger at the end. At the end, the culmination of the vision is in sight. You can see the outcome; you can see what you've been working towards. No, the danger of realizing any vision is right in the middle of the journey. It's right when you're not nearly finished and the start is as far away as the end. Germany proved the perfect metaphor for our journey as an organization so far. Starting something can be easy. Finishing something can be fun. The difficulty comes in battling day by day within the hard, oppressive environment of human trafficking; in difficult decisions, in sustained effort, in seeing something through. Yes, the danger is in the middle of the journey.

Then it started to rain. Of course it did! The wind picked up. The terrain became more difficult. I remember going around this corner and the view before me revealing itself almost as if in slow motion. Up until this moment, our path had been relatively flat, but as I turned this corner what I saw before me was what can only be described as, well, a mountain. We cycled nearer and nearer. And then, almost as if to tease us, we stopped for lunch at the bottom of the mountain. I gazed down at my lunch; I gazed up at the mountain. Suddenly even I'm not hungry any more. I walked over to speak to the guy who was planning our route.

'Hi, mate,' I said cautiously.

'Hi, Ben,' he replied.

'I'm just wondering . . .'

'Yes?'

'I'm just wondering, we are cycling *around* that mountain, right?'

And without even a flicker of emotion, he simply replied, 'Nope.'

'Great! Thanks, mate. That's cool. I love mountains.' I shrugged nonchalantly. Needless to say, that was a lie. I do not love mountains, not at all; and in that moment I couldn't imagine anything worse.

It was then that Isaac, our cameraman, decided to point the video camera at me and ask me to do a short clip to camera.

'Hey, Ben, tell me what's on your heart,' he said, with his normal dose of enthusiasm.

'You do not want to know what's on my heart right now, Isaac,' I thought, biting back the words. Tell me what's on your heart? And as I stood in the shadow of the mountain, camera pointed at my face, I started to sing:

'If faith could move the mountains, then let the mountains move.'

I turned around. The mountain was still there. I start again.

'If faith could move the mountains, then let the mountains move.'

I turned around again. That mountain isn't going anywhere. The mountain did not move.

That was the second thing our 'stint in the middle' taught me. Sometimes faith doesn't move the mountains; sometimes you are defined by your response to them. Whether you hold a particular faith or not, you may be expecting your circumstances to change, expecting your mountain to move before you do something. You may be sitting at the bottom of the mountain of slavery, poverty or fear or addiction, waiting for that mountain to move. But in reality we need to realize that we're stronger than we think we are; we're more able than our minds tell us we are.

When I first told people about Zoe's Hub and how we planned to fund it, people told me not to do it. They didn't think I could. I know that many of you might look at me and think I'm a healthy specimen of a human being (right!?), but before this challenge I did tests – health checks – and they appeared to suggest otherwise! The same tests that revealed that Tom (the actor) was incredibly fit, also revealed that Ben Cooley (the activist) was incredibly fat. I'm not exaggerating: they actually said I had a 'fat heart'. Already sceptical, my fat heart was the last straw. Cycle across Europe? People told me I simply wasn't able.

Maybe you can relate. There might be many people around you telling you that you're not able to achieve great things in your life. Let me tell you: you can climb that mountain, you're stronger than you think you are. I have learned that I am stronger than I think I am. Often I sit in boardrooms feeling totally intimidated because my education isn't right, because my age isn't right, because my accent isn't right or my credentials aren't right. Sometimes we wear those things as badges displaying the reasons why we can't do something. But you are stronger than you think you are. You have more potential than you realize and you can achieve more than you could ever imagine. How did I get to the top of the mountain? One pedal at a time. How are we going to end slavery? One life at a time. How are we going to end poverty? One person at a time. I firmly believe that we as a generation need to stop discounting ourselves, stop sitting at the bottom of the mountain. Rather we need to get up and start pedalling.

A few days later we were still in Germany which, as it turns out, is also a big country! We were cycling away and the wind had changed. Before this challenge, I didn't think the wind changing was a big deal, but it makes quite a difference. Who knew? Two or three days before this we were riding 22 miles per hour, but on this day we were putting in the same energy and going 6 miles per hour. The wind made a difference. We were hitting mountain after mountain, doing 12,000-foot climbs in a day. We were seriously disheartened. I was tired; my back hurt; my legs burned.

Then we hit this one particularly steep mountain. It was a 23% incline that quite literally went on for miles. I was in so much pain I was screaming out loud. I don't know what I was screaming, but all I can say is that if you happened to be in the middle of the German mountains and heard what I yelled, well I'm sorry. I was ready to give up. I was angry. I hated cycling. But I wasn't cycling because I like cycling; I was cycling because I wanted to make a difference. As much as my passion for rescuing victims such as Zoe and Emma had inspired me to take on the challenge, with both the start and end of the journey nowhere in sight, the burden felt too much to bear. I had nothing left.

There have been many times like this in my life. I remember one time when I, my wife and my kids had to move out of our home for a short time because of a threat to our safety. I remember sitting in my office with Gareth, one of our team, and feeling a similar thing: I'd had enough. I couldn't see how we would carry on. It was too much. You may have experienced something similar: you may have the vision, you may have the passion, but you're at a point at which it just hurts too much. That's where I was. It wasn't just about cycling. I felt the pressure of the whole future of Hope for Justice weighing on me; the responsibility of opening the new hub, of rescuing more people, of funding it all, felt as if it was on my shoulders. I was trying to carry it all myself, and I didn't have the strength.

I find the story of Moses in the Bible a great source of comfort. Moses had also got to a point at which the burden he had to carry was just too much to bear. He ended up just shouting at God and saying: 'God, I just can't carry it any more. It's too much for me.'

And God spoke to him: 'I understand. I see that you are hurting. Choose some of the leaders around you who can share the burden and I will take some of the same spirit that is on you and give it to them too and they will help you carry the load.' You know, as I was on this mountain, and I was just about to give up, I felt a hand on my shoulder. I turned and I looked behind me. And there was Jim, one of the cyclists. At that moment I felt another hand on my other shoulder: it was Gav, another of the cycling team. They were both cycling one-handed, with their other hands on my back, pushing me up the mountain.

I learned something in that moment – that some mountains are not meant to be climbed alone, that they're meant to be climbed with others. The vision of Hope for Justice, the vision to see the abolition of modern-day slavery, cannot be achieved by one individual. This mountain of the end of slavery can only become a reality if we climb it together, one hand on one another's backs, pushing towards the summit. On your own you're always less effective than if you're working in a team. This mountain is far too important for us to be walking alone. In those moments I learned that not only can I not climb it alone, actually I don't want to climb it alone.

We continued to cycle through Germany. And though, looking back, this pain was trivial and fleeting in comparison with the cause, in that moment I felt as if I were dying. The weather was terrible and physically I was now broken; mentally I was broken. I felt so cold that the team around me was actually beginning to think I was getting hypothermia. I had some weird conversations in those moments. I remember Tom asked me: 'How are you doing, man?'

'Menorca', I replied.

Now, I knew he had asked me how I was doing. So to answer with the name of one of Spain's Balearic islands was all the proof anyone needed that I was broken. That, and the fact I was blue. I was being sick eight or nine times a day. I couldn't keep food or water down.

Here's something you need to know about me: I love Nutella. My team know I love Nutella. Anyone who knows me knows I love Nutella. They also knew that past halfway, the journey would be hard. The office team sent us a video every day and that day I received a video that said 'Hey, Ben, you're awesome; you're doing an awesome job. We thought you might need a lift, so we have given Isaac some Nutella to give to you. Enjoy it!' Isaac was shaking his head. He had given me the Nutella on day two. I was in *that* place, that *dark* place on day two. This was day nine. There was no amount of Nutella that could bring me back from *this*.

I remember cycling next to Tom and him turning to me: 'Ben, you have got to control this pain.' I would love to say this was a purely benevolent act on his part but it might also have had something to do with the fact that I was screaming in his ear. I was really screaming. I know that may sound dramatic, but you have to remember that I trained as an opera singer; dramatic comes pretty naturally to me!

Tom continued: 'Mate, let me give you a tip about pain control, all right? What they do in the SAS is they teach you to build a wall around the pain.'

I cycled for a few minutes. I was thinking: 'All right, build a wall around the pain.' Build a wall. Around the pain.

'Tom,' I said, trying desperately hard to construct a wall mentally.

'Yes, Ben,' he replied, full of hope: was it working?

'I can't build a wall in real life, never mind an imaginary wall around my pain. How the heck do I build a wall around my body – in fact my soul – because my soul is in pain?'

Yes, my soul was in pain. That's how dramatic I felt. Everything within me had given up.

I've felt like that many times when I experienced hardships on the Hope for Justice journey. I imagine you have known the feeling in your own life, in your own mission. That moment when you're not just physically tired but mentally, emotionally and spiritually tired. And at that point your soul hurts.

Well, here was that feeling again. I was at that point. I was done. I stopped cycling. I started freewheeling through this town. Almost immediately Tom noticed. He saw that I'd stopped cycling. He started shouting at me:

'BEN! BEN!'

'What, Tom? I'm done. I'm finished.'

'Ben! Have you seen the town that we are cycling through?'

My head was down; disengaged.

Tom shouts again: 'Ben! Look up!'

Although I lacked the energy, I managed to raise my head. I looked up. And through my bleary eyes I saw the name of the town: Artern.

'Ben. It's Artern. It's *our turn*. It's *our time*. Don't you dare give up. You're not cycling for you, you're cycling for Zoe, you're cycling for Emma, you're cycling for every victim we've rescued and every victim we're still to rescue. It's our turn, Ben, it's our time.'

It's our turn. It's our time. We are the generation who will see an end to slavery.

There was my motivation. There was my 'why'. At times like this, whether it be on a bike in the middle of Germany or in an office making strategic decisions, it isn't the 'what' that motivates. It never is. It's the 'why'. Why do we do this? We do this because we believe every life counts.

Suddenly, there on the bike, with nothing left to give, I found my energy. This was not a physical energy: my soul had been re-energized because I rediscovered my purpose. Remember the 'why'. If you've started a project; if you've started something, anything; if you're in the thick of it, in the middle of it, I want to encourage you to write out your 'why's. Write down *why* you started. Write down *why* you care. Write down your vision. And then go back to it. Read it again and again. Because when I remembered my 'why', it propelled me. It energized me. It kept me going. We got through Germany. We got through Holland. We got through England. And I crossed the finish line and stood on the stage. Why? Because I remembered my purpose. Vision and purpose get you through. They can get you through that difficult time. They can get you through when you can't see the other side. They can get you through being sick eight times a day so you still get up the next morning. You can go through the pain and the agony of the journey. Why? Because what you do makes a difference. I have realized that it *is* our turn. Our generation is going to go through some pretty tough experiences. All around the world, people are being persecuted. There are political problems, economic problems and social problems that we'll have to face. But I tell you this now: we're going to see our vision become a reality if we remember our 'why'. We will achieve it if we remember our purpose. That's what that day taught me. I now face difficulties with a different attitude. I have a different mentality. I've been put on this earth for a purpose. So have you. I believe every person has a purpose. If you don't think you have a purpose, change your thinking. We all have a purpose; and that purpose could change the course of history.

ANOTHER SIDE TO THE STORY
TOM LISTER, ACTOR AND HOPE FOR JUSTICE
AMBASSADOR

I remember walking past a stand at the Men's Conference in Life Church Bradford and stopping: Hope for Justice. Up to this point I had been involved in several charity challenges, all for great causes, but I just felt like there was something missing. I had got really into the events (maybe because I was trying to stop myself from becoming a fat dad or had just got a taste for wearing Lycra?), but there was no real heart connection for me. I wanted to find something I was really passionate about, something I could invest my time and energy in. I walked past the Hope for Justice stand and knew this could be it. I walked up to the guy on the stand and said: 'Look, I'm interested in what you guys are about. If there is anything I can do to help, just get in touch.'

From there, I ended up going for a coffee with Ben. As soon as we sat down I felt like I'd known him for years. When he started to talk to me about Hope for Justice and the people they had rescued, it was almost like the scales started to fall from my eyes. Five or six years ago we hadn't really heard about human trafficking; it wasn't something that was in the public consciousness. I couldn't comprehend that this stuff was happening. I knew it was probably happening somewhere in the world, but it had felt like something quite distant from me. As Ben told me Zoe's story, I felt something inside me break. I felt as though this was what I needed to get involved in; this was what I needed to give my heart to. A couple of stories, lattes and muffins later I was, like, 'Right, what can I do? I'm in.'

Though I was busy working on the television soap opera *Emmerdale* at the time, I went to every Hope for Justice event I could. And when my time on the show came to an end, it was the perfect time to really get stuck into something and show my support. Pretty quickly Zoe's Challenge was born; and the 'support' had to come into play pretty quickly! I had already done lots of training for my charity events beforehand, but Ben *hates* cycling; in fact he doesn't even like exercise! And he needed to train for the event at the same time as running this huge organization. It came to the point where I would go over to help him train and be, like, 'If you ride up this hill, we'll take you to the pub and you can have some sticky toffee pudding.' He'd think about it, and then slowly nod: 'All right then, all right then.' Fast-forward half an hour and he'd be chundering all over his handlebars: 'Just think about that sticky toffee, Ben. It's right there at the top of the hill. It's waiting for you! Just picture it!'

Then the training was over and we were doing it for real. Setting off, I was so excited; but the fact that where we were starting was only fifty miles from the Russian border made it hard to ignore the size of what we were about to take on. It was pretty much continental Europe, from one side to the other. But the biggest challenge wasn't the size, it was the boredom! Maybe it was because we weren't having any rest days, but sometimes we'd be on these roads where it was so long and flat that it was like a never-ending horizon. Something Ben often quotes is that if we are going to make a real significant difference in fighting human trafficking, 'we don't need spasms of passion, we need long obedience in the same direction'. Nineteen days of cycling a hundred miles a day from one side of Europe to the other? It certainly felt like committing to sustained obedience to achieve an agreed goal!

I found Zoe's Challenge difficult, getting up every day to do a hundred miles when your backside is sore, your legs are tired and it's raining, so you know you're going to start a twelve-hour day wet from the start. It was miserable. And I like cycling! Ben doesn't like cycling in any form whatsoever. He would get up in the morning, we'd hit the road and he'd throw up within the first hour. It was grim. Maybe it was all those years spent watching funny YouTube videos of people being sick coming back to haunt him!

Then we got to Germany, and things really started to get tough. When we were in those moments it was just about getting alongside him and giving him a push. But no matter how hard he found it, he refused to get in the van and give up. He was, like, 'I won't do it. I don't want to be that guy; I don't want to be the fat little friend who sits in the van!' I kept saying: 'Mate! How can you say that? You've already cycled four countries across Europe. You can't say that now!' But no matter what Ben tells you, it wasn't always him: we all went through our own dips in energy. We only ever went as fast as our slowest rider; we were doing this together.

Ben's determination through the challenge was a real window into just how passionate he is about it. He knew what Zoe had gone through. He was, like, 'I've got to keep going, I've got to keep going for all the Zoes we haven't rescued yet!' He got through it for them. Returning to the UK, it was amazing: we had fifty to sixty riders joining us a day. It was really special. We were raising the profile of Hope for Justice and shedding light on human trafficking. But there is one thing Zoe said that will always stick in my mind. She said: 'I didn't need somebody to be aware of me, I needed somebody to do something. I needed somebody to do something to help me, and Hope for Justice did that. They came and found me, they rescued me.' Awareness alone is not enough to save someone.

Through Zoe's Challenge we were able to raise £250,000. Now we have a team in the West Midlands who have rescued hundreds of people, and will continue to do so. We want to plant more hubs. We're now operating internationally. The growth has been huge and the influence is great, but it's not enough if there are still people who are caught up in slavery. We're not at the end of our story yet, but I'm so privileged to be a part of it. We've come a long way since our first coffee together, but I still look at Ben and I'm, like, 'Come on, mate. What's next? Let's get back in those trenches and see what we can achieve together.'

USE
YOUR VOICE.

IT COULD CHANGE
SOMEONE'S LIFE
FOR EVER.

Chapter nine

WILLIAM AND SAMUEL'S STORY

Five years is a long time. It was for William. That's at least as long as he was locked into a cycle of exploitation, moved from city to city across the UK. Every day, ordinary people passed by the house where he was painting and plastering for no pay, at the hands of violent traffickers. He looked like a legitimate labourer. But the reality could not be further from the truth.

The conditions William was made to eat and sleep in were subhuman; there were rooms full of others who were being similarly exploited. Body after body forced to live, eat and sleep in cramped conditions. William was a strong man. He felt ashamed that he had allowed himself to end up in this situation, but he also felt trapped.

After a few years he met Samuel. Samuel seemed like a kindred spirit. They would talk occasionally, when they found a moment out of earshot of the traffickers. It was during one such discussion that they agreed that together they would try to survive. They went on the run.

They were frightened; they were tired and unable to afford transport out of the area; they lived in constant fear of being found.

When William's trafficker caught up with them they were locked in properties to work all day. The trafficker's fury was unleashed and at one point they were made to sleep on the freezing floor of the trafficker's basement. During some of the coldest weather either of the men had experienced, William fell ill from the damp. Because of his worsening condition, the traffickers wanted to monitor William more closely and he was allowed to sleep on the floor in the main house. Eventually William's health improved and he and Samuel began talking again. They had to escape. This was no life for them. They would rather die trying to flee the evil they were enduring than live like this for the remainder of their existence. So once again they ran.

This time the traffickers did not find them. William and Samuel were constantly on edge. They could not relax. They could not sleep. But what kept them going was the knowledge of what they had escaped from. They ended up living on the streets. Even though their existence was hard, they knew they had done the right thing. Hope for Justice identified William and Samuel on the streets after a referral was made to our specialist team by an organization we had trained. The Hope for Justice team made sure the pair were put up in a safe house; they were given clothing, food, but most importantly they were given hope. This intervention meant they no longer needed to live in fear of their traffickers.

FAMILY MATTERS

Zoe's Challenge was complete. Emma's Hub was flying. The second hub was ready to open. We had thousands of regular givers, hundreds of Abolition Groups. I was even being invited to speak on big platforms and television shows! I remember one of the first times the BBC asked to interview me; it was for BBC News 24, their national twenty-four-hour news channel. I was shown into a room; there was no-one else there. The lady who had shown me in drew the curtains, sat me down and gave me an earpiece. She left. And I was, like, 'So when does this start?' Thankfully I wasn't doing anything embarrassing like sorting my hair or scratching my nose because then suddenly in my ear was a 'Three, two, one; and here is Ben Cooley from Hope for Justice.' Thanks to media interviews like this (and the many opportunities that have come our way since), we started to generate significant critical mass as a movement.

At this point in our journey, people may have looked at me and thought: 'Wow, look at Ben. He must be more confident than ever. More successful.' But as I've said before, there is often a real loneliness in leadership. This point, after opening our third UK office, was the ultimate in loneliness for me. It was partly down to having such an intense experience as a team as part of the Zoe Challenge. But it was also that I had never felt so scared because now we had built something, now we had profile, I really felt the weight of the responsibility and of getting this right. I would be absolutely petrified going on television. I remember going into studios shaking with fear.

I've realized that when people have profile, when they are up front or on a stage, we all assume things about that individual. We think that person is confident or maybe even wish we could be on the stage ourselves. I don't believe what I go through is any different from what you go through. Life happens. Difficulties are always there. Stages and profile do not change that. We all have struggles. We all have challenges. In those moments of fear, I've had to go back to that 'mountain moment' in Germany and remind myself that I'm stronger than I think I am in order to combat them. I've had to learn to be comfortable being scared. I've had to learn not to let my fear make decisions for me; rather, I'm going to make decisions despite the anxiety.

I'm nervous most of the time when using my voice. I've gone through crises of confidence in how I deliver a message. In those moments I think of Martin Luther King. I bet when he stood on that platform he was anxious too. The political environment, the danger to his and his family's safety would have been frightening. He did it anyway. I'm sure that for Nelson Mandela, in his fight against apartheid, there would have been times just before he stepped on to a stage – and maybe a death threat had been received or the crowds became unruly – when he was fearful. But he did it anyway. Now I'm not comparing myself to Martin Luther King or to Nelson Mandela. But for my inspiration I am looking up to great people who are scared of what they are about to face but who do it anyway. It is the lives of great leaders, including that of Jesus, that have taught me this. You are going to come across things that terrify you. But you should get on with it anyway.

One of the reasons I get nervous is because I often feel I don't fit the bill. I represent a serious cause. And of course, when I talk about it, I am serious about it. But if you ask any of my close friends, I love making people laugh. I love humour. Humour and serious work should not be mutually exclusive. I don't think because I love to laugh that I can't work to abolish human trafficking. We all need to laugh. Laughter is a great benefit to us individually and corporately. Joy and laughter are a necessary antidote to some of the things we're exposed to while fighting for such a heartbreaking cause. For some people this means I can be difficult to understand. Sometimes I'm seen as this crazy individual, someone who is intense, who is passionate about something incredibly serious; but the next minute someone who is laughing and cracking jokes.

And yet for every person who isn't able to make you out, there is someone determined to put you in a box. That's one of the difficult things I've faced with media, being pigeonholed: I'm the voice on human trafficking to a lot of people. Now don't get me wrong: I'm seriously passionate about ending human trafficking, but there's a lot more I'm also passionate about. I don't always sit nicely in the category people have placed me in. Perhaps you can relate to this. However you have been positioned, however you are perceived and however scared you might be, remember to use your voice. It could change someone's life for ever.

I've realized that one of the reasons certain people achieve success – whether they are founders of organizations, CEOs or simply extremely ambitious – is because they are absolutely, even ruthlessly, dedicated to their mission. Of course, that is important. Vitally important. But sometimes we forget that we may adopt many roles in our lives. And sometimes the focus that offers success in an organization has the capacity to distract and even distort your view on other aspects of your life, such as friendships and family.

If I am honest, I hadn't realized I'd become this ruthlessly focused person until one day I had a meeting with a guy who led a large company. He understood business and had achieved much corporate acclaim. He was someone I hugely admired. He turned to me and said: 'How are your kids?'

I replied: 'Yes, the kids are doing great.' In my mind I was thinking: 'When do we get back to talking about the mission?'

He said: 'Ben, can I share the best piece of advice I have ever been given? This is the pattern that will emerge with your kids:

five, ten, fifteen, gone; and how they "go" is how they will stay for the rest of their lives.'

It took a while for the truth of this to sink in. It probably wasn't even in that meeting that I got it, but I thought about it over the coming days and came to understand the importance of this truth.

Five, ten, fifteen, gone.

It led me to ask myself some serious questions. Not what kind of CEO I wanted to become; rather, 'What kind of man do I want to become? Do I want to be a good father? Do I want to be a good husband? Do I want to be a good friend?'

I'm not saying I've got this completely right and that I'm now the perfect dad and perfect husband, but I have realized over the years that family takes priority and the importance of being a father, of going to the dance recitals, the swimming lessons and the Christmas show, no matter what the work schedule looks like. I've discovered that it's essential to make sure your wife knows that, when you are away on another work trip, you miss her. I've seen so many mission-minded people forget that their family was always a part of their mission.

I'm committed more than ever to quality time together, to great holidays together, to having ice creams together and to dreaming big together. I'm determined that my kids should get to see their father, and ever since I came to this realization I've seen our family bond closer together than we ever have. There's a lot to be said for the sacrifice my children and my wife make to enable the abolition of the modern-day slave trade: doing without material things, sometimes doing without time with Dad.

The team that we are, Team Cooley, is stronger than ever.

I want to end slavery, but I don't believe that needs to be at the expense of my family.

When my kids have hit five, ten, fifteen, and have gone to live their own lives, I'm sure now that they'll go knowing the love and support of their parents and believing they can achieve their dreams.

ANOTHER SIDE TO THE STORY
DEB COOLEY, CO-FOUNDER OF HOPE FOR JUSTICE

Leaving that first presentation by Rob and Marion White in Manchester Town Hall, I remember being incredibly moved and thinking: 'Wow, this tour could be the start of something incredible.' At that point I didn't really personalize it, I didn't think: 'Now I need to do something.' But Ben was different. The message had hit him like a bullet between the eyes. He felt it very personally. He felt he needed to do something about it. Weeks later the vision of The Stand was born.

The personal cost of putting on the event was all mashed up with the whole situation we were in at the time. Ben was recently graduated and part self-employed, and I was on maternity leave. And yet I felt filled with a childlike faith that if God was in it, it would all be all right. Then the night came. Standing on that stage, speaking to the crowd who'd come to be with us, it was just incredibly overwhelming. I remember looking over at Ben and thinking: 'Wow, people are with us.' I remember feeling really proud of the church in that moment. Ben and I had always believed in the power of the church, that we should be a people leading the way against injustice, speaking out and not staying silent. At The Stand this was confirmed for us all over again.

The Stand was an incredible night. We highlighted all of these wonderful organizations who had come and partnered with us. We were able to give an opportunity to these amazing causes and say to others; 'Come on, look at what these guys are doing. It's really good. Get involved with them!'

Then the question came: 'All right, what do we do next?' What do we do with people wanting to give money to us? We'd had to create an organization and give it a name by this point, but I don't think any of us imagined that Hope for Justice was going to be what it is now. Even after the event, I don't think we thought: 'This is what we're going to do now: we're going to step into the whole area of human trafficking and bring it down; this is going to be our fight.' I don't think any of us really thought that Hope for Justice was going to suddenly grow legs and arms and begin to run.

But Hope for Justice has never run alone. The same heart for partnership that we presented at The Stand has stayed with us through our entire journey. In everything we've done then and since, we've tried to create something that shows people that it's possible to work together and that charities don't have to be in competition with one another, that they can actually be companions not competitors. For me, that's the saddest thing we encounter, not just with Christians but with people of any faith and none. Such damage can be caused by acting in a way that suggests we're in competition with each other and that one is better than another; there is such damage in thinking: 'If you do well that means we're not doing well, therefore we don't want you to do well.' All of that is so distracting, energy zapping and fruitless that we have made it one of the hallmarks of our organization to demonstrate to the church, the charity world, to governments, to organizations and agencies that it is entirely possible to work together. And not only possible but preferable, because the results are far superior when you do work together. That is what we would love to see: more partnerships and replication of what we see working in many other countries.

We're trying to build a movement not a moment. We want to create a movement because a movement continues long after the original movers have finished and long after they've gone. At Hope for Justice, our dream is ultimately to end slavery, but we also want to do ourselves out of a job! We want to be able to move on to something else because we have seen an end to slavery.

ENCOURAGE ONE ANOTHER DAILY.

Chapter ten

MA NI'S STORY

Every little girl should be allowed to play, to dance, to laugh. Every little girl should feel loved. For Ma Ni, childhood was a very different story.

Growing up, this little girl was ruthlessly exploited for labour by a family member. She rarely saw friends or played games. Instead she was forced to work relentless hours. She lived in Cambodia's Battambang Province with an abusive father, and her family were scarcely able to afford one meal a day. They were sometimes so desperate they had to scavenge for food or beg their neighbours to feed them. This was barely an existence, never mind a childhood. As Ma Ni grew up, she wished for a better future in Thailand.

One day a customer offered her a much better job across the border, as a house cleaner. With nowhere else to turn and desperate to escape her exploitation, she jumped at the opportunity. But soon after her journey started, her life became a living nightmare. She had been sold to traffickers. One of the men raped her many times. The next morning she was sold on, to another man. Her body was used to pleasure men twice and three times her age. She was in torture. All she had wanted was a better life, all she had wanted was to earn a living and make a future for herself. Now she felt worthless and alone.

Taking a rare an unexpected opportunity, Ma Ni managed to escape and found her way back to Cambodia. She didn't know where she was running to, but she certainly knew what she was running from. Whatever the future held, it had to be better than the darkness she was fleeing.

The police eventually found Ma Ni and brought her to a Hope for Justice safe house for restoration. She was so scared at first that she couldn't even sleep. She had so many nightmares about what had happened to her. Night after night the faces of her abusers would appear in her mind. Grinning, sweaty, dirty men. She would blame herself for everything that happened to her. She felt such a deep sense of guilt and shame. But over time things began to change. Through Hope for Justice programmes, therapy and treatment, day by day, Ma Ni got better.

Ma Ni later shared: 'Coming to Hope for Justice was a turning point for my life. My life is filled with hope now. I feel like I know what I want my future to look like.' It is a future filled with hope.

BETTER TOGETHER

Ma Ni's story was an amazing one but it actually wasn't one of ours. It was a story from a Cambodian anti-trafficking charity called Transitions Global. You see, there were other organizations that shared the same goal we had, which was to see the end of modern-day slavery for good. Transitions Global were working with another agency and our friend Stacia Freeman. Stacia worked for Abolition International and it was she who asked the question: 'Why are we doing this alone?' Abolition International had

had separate talks with Transitions Global (which we had supported through our financial giving programme), and out of those conversations came the bold proposal that we all become one organization.

Passionate, positive and all sharing a common purpose, the three of us agreed to continue and develop the conversation in what would turn out to be an incredible process. We all decided to lay down our agendas because the need to end human trafficking was far greater than the need to promote our individual organizations.

I remember one evening: I was on the phone to Natalie Grant, founder of Abolition International. Here I am speaking with this unbelievable woman, an internationally renowned, Grammy-nominated singer, and the voice on the end of the phone tells me that she would be happy to lose her brand name because the people we were looking to rescue were more important. That was the spirit of the merger. It wasn't about who got what. It was about how we build something that will more effectively see an end to human trafficking globally. The merger increased our capacity. Together we were stronger.

The process of merging is always a challenge, but it is one of the best things we have done as an organization. Through merging with Transitions Global in Cambodia, founded by James and Athena Pond (who went on to lead our Cambodian Hope for Justice office), we have acquired experts in aftercare, which is something we have never had in the UK before. Through Stacia and her team we were able to learn more about training and the issues around child sexual exploitation in the USA. We are now better equipped than ever to see an end to modern-day slavery. If you decide to merge, you have to be of the right mindset. I'm so proud of everyone involved in this merger because it wasn't about position, it was about legacy. We believed that our joint legacy of freedom would be far greater than anything we might achieve separately.

I'll never forget about a week or so before we announced the merger when I was having dinner with James and Athena in Cambodia after a day of filming. As we talked and laughed together, I just got this overwhelming sense of pride. This couple had given up all the comfort and convenience of the USA to work in the hot, sticky and challenging environment of Cambodia. They had sacrificed so much and all because they believed in the fight against modern-day slavery and the vision to see victims restored.

Only a week later, we launched at an event called Night of Freedom. I was backstage talking to Natalie, and I'll never forget how humble she was as we said a little prayer together. I felt so proud to stand alongside her and continue to feel so to this day. Exactly the same with Stacia, James and Athena. In our hearts we are all Abolitionists. The three organizations became Hope for Justice. Their story is our story but you should probably hear it from them.

NATALIE'S STORY
NATALIE GRANT, SINGER, SONGWRITER AND
CO-FOUNDER OF HOPE FOR JUSTICE (INTL.)

I remember the first time I became aware of modern-day slavery. It was 2004 and I had been on tour as part of my work as a contemporary Christian recording artist. It was my day off and I was at home watching one of my favourite TV shows, *Law and Order* – it's a fictional show but they say that every episode is based on factual cases from the headlines. The episode I saw depicted children being sold as sex slaves in New York City. They showed several kids being held in the basement of a Manhattan apartment; I remember thinking, 'Which headline has this been ripped from? This is not real. This is not happening.'

At the end of the episode, I googled, 'What is human trafficking?' Although not many people were talking about the issue back then, I found a document published by the US government called the *Trafficking in Persons Report*. I don't think I understood half of it but I understood enough to realize that human trafficking was real, that slavery still existed and most slaves in the world were children.

Soon afterwards, I found an organization involved in combating slavery; I called its toll-free number and said, 'This is going to sound crazy but I am a singer. I stand on a stage and I feel like people need to know this is happening in the world.' I ended up going on a trip to India with my husband; I saw the red-light district at first hand. I'll never forget looking up at a second-storey window and seeing a little girl, no more than 6 years old, literally sitting in a cage. It was one of those moments in life when you are not really sure what you can do, you just know that you have to do something.

I came back from that trip determined to use my platform to make a difference. I started the process of creating my own non-profit organization to raise awareness about trafficking and slavery. That is how Abolition International came to be in 2005. I didn't have a clue what I was doing; I just wanted to address a huge injustice. Amazingly, some really incredible people crossed my path who were able to aid me in getting the charity off the ground.

In those early days, we had some wonderful trained medical professionals and psychologists who helped us to focus on our heart for restoration. Although we could see other organizations raising awareness, the statistics showed that, without good-quality care and the proper clinical training in place to restore individuals, over 90% of those rescued from slavery would return to being enslaved. It's hard for people who have never been victims to understand why on earth someone would ever go back to slavery after being freed. Yet there are deep psychological issues that have to be treated to ensure the cycle of slavery is broken. That's why we initially set our sights on writing manuals for standardized care.

Abolition International was fantastic but there was always a little piece missing. If I'm honest, I want to be the kind of person who could carry out a raid. I want to go in, get the bad guys and get all the kids out, but that is not part of my skill set. My greatest gift is that I have a platform in the public eye; people listen to me. Although I want to be involved in all the various aspects, I've had to learn that there are other people who have the right abilities and are able to use them far more effectively than I can. It is people like this, with the relevant training, experience and infrastructure, who would take the charity to the next level.

I first became aware of Hope for Justice through one of my dearest friends, Charlotte Gambill. I remember telling her about the passion I had to fight human trafficking. She said to me, 'Well, we have a really good friend called Ben Cooley who is doing incredible work here in the UK.' When I came over to England to meet Ben for the first time, I thought he was crazy – crazy, boisterous and loud – but I always say you have to be slightly crazy to make an incredible difference in the world; you have to be crazy enough to believe that you can. Ben has that belief. A lot of people will look at a situation and ask, 'Why?' Ben will look at it and ask, 'Why not? Why couldn't we do that? Why couldn't we change the world?'

It was from there that I began to learn what Hope for Justice does. The more I learned, the more I realized that what Abolition International had – my public platform and a way to raise the profile of human trafficking – was what Hope for Justice needed. And what Hope for Justice had – infrastructure from a professional standpoint – was what Abolition International needed. After all, without the ability to rescue victims, who are you providing restorative care for? Later, Hope for Justice introduced me to the wonderful Athena and James Pond and the amazing work of Transitions Global in Cambodia. The more we explored together, the more it seemed like a perfect match – that our three passionate organizations should become one.

Naturally, when we were talking about merging Abolition International, Hope for Justice and Transitions Global, there was the question of which name we were going to use. Honestly, in my humanity, that was a struggle for me at first. I thought, 'Wait a second! This is our name!' And yet, the moment you put your feelings to one side, you realize an issue is so much bigger than someone's pride or agenda – all that matters to our charities is that we free as many people as possible and restore them to a better life, a hope and a future. I've learnt over the years that non-profit work usually comes from a good place – the desire to help – but then people become involved and they can mess everything up! We all have our own agendas and our own ideas, and people's feelings can get hurt. It's very hard sometimes to put those things aside for the greater good. When you do, you soon realize that 'together is better' is more than just an optimistic phrase – it's a reality.

It is hard to find the people who are able to put their agendas aside and partner together but, when you do, there is such a great opportunity to make a difference; there is power in numbers.

Together you can accomplish so much more than you ever could apart. I remember being so excited about announcing the merger at Night of Freedom for that very reason. You hear a lot of people say, 'Together we can do this', then they all go back to their own corners of the world and get caught up in their own things. But here we were in Nashville, Tennessee, where everybody says 'y'all', and this guy with a strong British accent gets up to talk about fighting human trafficking. It was such a beautiful picture of the three organizations joining together on an international level to take on an international problem.

I believe our merger has really allowed me to put Abolition International into very capable hands, to let it to be carried by Ben, Athena, James and their teams, enabling me to go back to what I do best: using my platform to tell people how they can play a part in fighting slavery. There was such a lesson in it for me: sometimes we can hold on to our own ideas or goals too tightly. The tighter I held on to my dream, the more I stifled its growth; the more I let go of it, the more it grew, and I'm really grateful that I can trust Ben, Athena and James and the rest of the team. I know of their integrity; I know that action backs up their words. I long to see the work in Cambodia grow, and it is! I long to see the work in the USA grow, and that is happening as well. The progress is just slower than I want it to be; yet I know that slow and steady wins the race. Hope for Justice is tackling this issue in the right way, making sure it's work will last.

It's funny the way things become trendy – not just fashion but causes too; it's part of human nature to jump on a bandwagon! And right now it does seem that human trafficking has become a very trendy cause: people are making bracelets inscribed with slogans about it and writing red Xs on their hands. I'm not saying this to take anything away from these initiatives. In fact, I am so grateful that they are flourishing because, when a cause is on trend, the awareness becomes so massive that a lot is achieved. But what's important is that organizations are set up to handle their business in the right way. Then, when mainstream culture moves on to a different cause, they will still carry on the real work. That's what I believe about Hope for Justice. I believe in our work so strongly that I know – long after trends come and go – we will still be there doing the work, getting real results and seeing freedom come to so many more people. That's why I believe deeply in what we are doing – we are building something to last.

ANOTHER SIDE TO THE STORY
ATHENA POND, INTERNATIONAL PROGRAMME
OPERATIONS DIRECTOR AND CO-FOUNDER OF HOPE
FOR JUSTICE (INTL.)

James and I first heard about human trafficking in 2004, and our hearts were instantly broken at the thought of human beings – children – being sold for sex and profit. We knew we could not look away, could not hope that someone else would intervene, and so we began a journey to learn more about the problem and what we could do to help. In 2005 we chose to move to Phnom Penh, Cambodia, and start a long-term aftercare shelter with an organization there. We sold our house, our cars, most of our belongings, and left the USA with our three children, Ashley, 15, Gabriel, 13 and Alexis, 9 years old. This began a truly amazing adventure for us as a family and re-set the course of our lives for ever.

We knew nothing about running an aftercare facility for girls who had just been rescued from slavery, but we knew we could learn and we knew we were willing. As we began the work we quickly saw the need for a more professional, intensive, focused strategy that helped girls complete the transition back into society with viable life and job skills. We were committed to building a programme based on excellence and the ethos of everything we did for the girls in our care being what we would do for our own daughters. To achieve our goal, we moved back to the USA and started our own organization, Transitions Global, so we could create the holistic initiative we dreamed of.

With a major focus on this programme, we spent the next seven years travelling back and forth to Cambodia, building relationships in the community and a reputation for excellence in aftercare. Aside from our incredible Khmer staff and a few wonderfully dedicated volunteers, James and I did the work of creating programmes and running an international non-profit organization alone. We didn't have support staff, a marketing team or a development team, and it was very challenging to cover all those roles ourselves. There were very long work days, no time off for holidays or vacations, and the entire burden of keeping things going fell largely on us. It was a very long and lonely seven years!

Along this journey we met some great people in the fight to end modern-day slavery. Two of those people were Ben Cooley of Hope for Justice and Stacia Freeman of Abolition International. Ben and James had become friends in 2007 and spent many hours over Skype sharing the challenges of being CEOs and the work to help survivors find freedom. Stacia, James and I worked together towards seeing standards set for survivor care in the USA. As we grew closer through the years there was a lot of laughter, friendship and shared experiences, but most of all a common calling to see the end of slavery and the restoration of those rescued from it.

In 2013 Stacia started talking to us about increased collaboration and a sharing of strengths to make even greater impact. She asked us why we were each trying to do this alone when we could do so much more together. That really resonated with us and we all began to talk and think about what that kind of collaboration could look like. For James and I it would mean no longer running an organization alone. We would be free to focus on what we loved the most: programmes to help restore survivors. Ultimately we all decided we were better together, each organization bringing its own unique strengths and expertise, making one vibrant, larger organization. The merger didn't come without its growing pains, though, and the process is certainly not for the faint of heart. We had all built successful organizations and were all leaders in our own rights, each with an individual board of directors who had invested their time and talents in that success. It took a year of talking and planning and understanding what each organization could bring to the table before we were ready to move forward. The key was the willingness we all had to lay down our egos and personal desires for what we truly believed was important: changing lives and ending slavery.

What we were about to do was unprecedented in the anti-trafficking community, and when new organizations were continually appearing, we were about to dismantle our three organizations, restructure them as one and come out the other side more efficient and more effective. We all believed this was the right way forward, and an example of what collaboration could mean and accomplish. In September 2014 we announced the merger to the world, and came under the banner of Hope for Justice, three organizations becoming one. We each had a personal mandate in the fight against slavery, but I'm so thankful we chose to do more together. It's been a remarkable journey since then, and we've seen growth and opportunity in Cambodia and in every country where Hope for Justice works. I am excited to see what the future holds for this organization, the dedicated people within it and, most importantly, the survivors we serve.

I BELIEVE THAT WE CAN SEE EVERY LIFE SET FREE.

Chapter eleven

ELITA'S STORY

Elita grew up in Eastern Europe, where she had a tough start to life. Abused as a young child, Elita turned to alcohol to help her cope. She ended up homeless. While in this desperate situation she was approached and offered money to come to the UK and marry a man. With no other option, she agreed.

When Elita arrived in the UK, she found she had been tricked and was trafficked for the purposes of sexual exploitation and forced labour. She was locked up, raped and forced to have sex with many men. She was also forced to work in different jobs, and her trafficker took all the wages she earned. Elita's ID documents were taken from her to prevent her running away; she was assaulted and they threatened to kill her.

In an effort to cope with the trauma inflicted on her, Elita was drinking heavily. She made contact with a support service to help with this, and a worker recognized the signs of trafficking and contacted Hope for Justice. We were able to help her leave the cycle of exploitation and enter a safe house. However, rescue is not an event, it is a process. Elita needed a lot of support to recover from her traumatic experiences, and still struggled with alcohol.

When she left the safe house she relapsed. Hope for Justice met with her and, after a lot of hard work, and determination on Elita's part, she gave rehab another try and is now clean. She has found other ways to deal with her trauma, and is doing so well. Our team are so incredibly proud of her and how far she has come in a short time.

WE DON'T HAVE TIME

Following our merger with Abolition International and Transitions Global, I had shared with our staff that we were entering into a year of consolidation. A year to focus on health and not necessarily growth. A year to take stock. But we are a dynamic organization. We don't stop for long. Amazingly, we could do little to slow the momentum of the movement we had together worked so hard to create. I think in many ways our momentum has always been powered by a sense of urgency.

As much as we would love a year to slow down, to focus our efforts, often we are faced with the fact that we just don't have time. We don't have time to sit back and congratulate one another and become nostalgic about what we've achieved over the past period. We don't have time to be offended by things that have been done or not done. We don't have time to sit and navel-gaze. There has been that pressing need to act hanging over whatever we have done.

At Hope for Justice, we love our staff. It's a passion of ours, and particularly Debbie's, to care for our staff and make sure our team is supported and invested in; to make sure they feel valued, that they feel that their work is needed and encouraged. But there isn't time for us to go 'All right, this year needs to be an easy year now. We're not going to try as hard and we're not going to go after this or go after that because that will put too much pressure on us.' We can't think that way.

Often we're faced with an open door of opportunity that we didn't expect. Sometimes we don't know what it will lead to or how we'll make it work, but we know we're going to walk through it. There isn't time for us to hang about; too many people are still waiting for us to come. There are too many people who find themselves beyond our reach. There is just that sense that we don't have time to consolidate or to take time out from doing this or doing that. If the opportunity is there to grow or expand something, then we have to find a way to make that work. And that's a challenge, because we want to be sustainable. We don't want to over-promise and under-deliver. But we're all too aware of the urgency of the task at hand.

And so, mere weeks into our 'time of consolidation', the Lighthouse Project, which we had set up in collaboration with the government in Cambodia only months after the merger, was producing story after story of lives changed. Through the Lighthouse Project, Hope for Justice now received children who had been sexually abused from across the country for the first stages of their aftercare. What's more, this refusal to slow down was not confined to Cambodia alone, it was intensifying across the globe.

In the UK we have taken on more staff to help increase outreach and impact. In the USA we have employed some incredible people, including the former head of the anti-human trafficking programme within the FBI's Civil Rights Unit. I tried to make it a year of consolidation, but people shouldn't have to wait for their freedom. They can't wait for it, and we just can't wait to give it to them. I think some people may have been critical about our expansion. Some people asked if it means we will now give less focus to the UK. The answer is simply: no. Hope for Justice is absolutely, wholeheartedly committed to ending modern-day slavery in the UK. It's just that now our capacity has grown. When I became a father for the second time, there was simply no question about whether I would love my second daughter as much as my first. You don't love any less. Your capacity just changes. I am no less passionate about the abolition of the slave trade in the UK, but our capacity has grown. It now includes Cambodia, the USA, Norway and many other countries. Same passion; greater capacity. And with greater capacity comes a greater platform: a *global* platform. So the question is: What is Hope for Justice going to do now?

Well, the last thing we want to do is use the platform simply to communicate a message, to be all talk and no action, all words and no substance. Many people have inspired me throughout my life: people I've known personally; people I've read about and studied, whether that's Mother Teresa or the founder of the Salvation Army, William Booth, or Martin Luther King, who inspired a generation to stand up to injustice. Many have inspired me with incredible visions, and I am so grateful to all those people who have stood on platforms and used their voices for things that matter. But what's the one thing all of these people had in common? They didn't just use their voices for communication but for creation.

I believe our generation should use its voice not just to *communicate* about injustice but also to create a solution, to inspire people, to motivate them to move beyond the confines of their own lives and to use their lives to transform others. To use their freedom to bring freedom to others. To use their resources to empower others. To do more, be more, achieve more. It may be that you're not being oppressed yourself, but millions of people are being oppressed all across the world. They are in our supply chains. They are being held against their will for forced labour, domestic servitude and sexual exploitation. There are slaves in our country and countries all over the world, and they are waiting for someone to use their voice, to use their voice to prompt action, use their message to inspire mission.

In some ways this book is a letter from me to you. Let me ask you: Why don't you join us? Why don't you join with us to see the true abolition of the slave trade become a reality? Not just to talk about it or even just cry about it, but to see how we actually free every slave. We believe that freedom is worth the fight. We believe justice is non-negotiable. We refuse to abandon the least, the last and the lost. We choose to challenge apathy with action. We choose to greet cynicism with hope. We are purposeful, passionate and pioneering. We are Hope for Justice. This book is not the solution in itself but my hope would be that it could be a part of it. It's a conversation between me and you, an invitation to be a part of this movement. I believe we can see an end to slavery.

I believe that we can see every life set free. The world I see is a world where children are free to live, free to play, free to dance. Not bound by a man's lust, not attacked by a predator who is seeking to exploit them. The world I see is a world in which women are valued and have honour, a world in which men speak well of them; men who won't degrade women or abuse them and force them to service man after man against their will.

The world I see is a world where men are able to provide for their families and are not forced to work digging holes without tools in freezing conditions, where their fingers break and hands are deformed. They are not locked in a cellar for years and years in disgusting and inhumane conditions. The world I see does not have families broken by this hideous crime. It does not see businesses profiting from exploitation. It is full of people who are not complicit or apathetic but who take a stand.

The world I see is a world free from slavery. Frequently, Tim Nelson and I dream of a time, maybe in our later years, when we can sit on a beach and play backgammon and talk about the moment slavery ended for good. And that's the world I want to live in. People may look at me and think I am ill equipped or simply unable to do this. But I'm going to die trying. Because I would rather live in my preferable future than in a reality in which my brothers and sisters are being bought and sold for profit. If you believe what I believe, if you see what I see, then join us.

Muhammad Ali once said:

> Impossible is just a big word thrown around by small men who find it easier to live in the world they've been given than to explore the power they have to change it.
> Impossible is not a fact. It's an opinion.
> Impossible is not a declaration. It's a dare.
> Impossible is potential.
> Impossible is temporary.
> Impossible is nothing.

Here's my dare to you:

- I dare you to end trafficking;
- I dare you to use your freedom to free others;
- I dare you to stand with us to see the abolition of the slave trade.

ANOTHER SIDE TO THE STORY
ELITA, VICTIM OF HUMAN TRAFFICKING AND
RESCUEE OF HOPE FOR JUSTICE

When I look back on my first encounter with Hope for Justice, everything is a bit foggy. When I first received a visit from Naomi, a member of the Hope for Justice Team, I wasn't sure what to think. I felt completely alone, with no clothes, no money, no hope. I thought everyone had forgotten about me and I was really on my own. I was just existing. I didn't have any self-worth at all. I didn't know someone could care about me, think anything good about me. I felt like the worst person in the world and like I should just disappear from the planet.

A support worker from another charity said she would help find me a team who could help, but I didn't believe anyone would want to help. I had nothing; I had burned through all my options. I didn't know where to go for help. But Naomi and other people helped me and things started to change. It's hard to keep helping someone who is drunk, but Naomi did. My drinking was a symptom of trauma; I couldn't just stop through willpower. That's why they encourage support groups. You just can't do it on your own.

After a period of recovery I fell back into drinking and thought my life would finish there; I wasn't able to live with myself for even one day. I couldn't cope any more; it was too much, too heavy. While I was in hospital Naomi just started things moving, connecting me to all these people who could help. I didn't need to do anything really. I just needed to trust. After feeling so alone in this country and not knowing who to turn to, it was amazing not to feel on my own any more.

I remember the day when Hope for Justice rang me to say that they could sort out a place for me to stay. I'd been staying in B & Bs, but I had to move because of my drinking and behaviour. I was on the street and I didn't know what to do. I was in a very hopeless situation. I had nothing. I didn't want to drink any more, I didn't even want to kill myself, I was just at the end. But somehow there was this strength, and then Naomi rang me, and I couldn't believe I had a place to stay.

Somehow, from having nothing, I found the strength and motivation and hope and power to move forward to something better. It's kind of magical, when you go that far down and get back up again. So many times in my life I've tried to get back on my feet, but it's very difficult when you lose everything and have no-one to help you. I'm very proud that I've been able to get up from where I was, from such a dark place.

Now I just have to take things one day at a time. I don't want to put big expectations on my future right now because it's all too uncertain. I would love to stay in the UK, but there are loads of legal things related to my trafficking experience and so on that I need to sort out, and it's not something I can do in a day. In the future I would really like to go to college and study, and personally I would like to give something back to the community, to the society that helped me. I would definitely like to be something like a support worker and help others. I want to help people get out of dark situations, and show them it's possible! I know it takes time; I don't want to rush, but eventually that's what I really want to do: help others like I have been helped.

If I encountered someone who had been through what I've been through or was in a similarly dark place, I would tell them not to lose their hope, the hope that there is help somewhere that will come at the right time. Don't give up, be patient and keep fighting. It sometimes feels hard but definitely never give up, whatever happens. There are organizations and individuals that can help you. It can be hard to find the right help and sometimes you feel you're being passed from one place to the other, but you need to keep in mind that however much you're destroyed, you deserve the right help. You are worth something. You have the right to be treated like a normal human being. Everyone deserves a life. It's so easy to forget, but don't lose hope: find something you believe in. I don't show my faith to many people because it's private, but it's been a massive support to me.

Don't let anyone judge you for the mistakes you've made, because we are all human beings. I need to be responsible and make amends, but no human being can put me down. Nobody is worth less or more. We are all the same and have the same rights. Look forward, to every new moment. It's very easy to forget about the small things, and then you don't see them any more. But the small things are the most important, the most beautiful. Like when you wake up in the morning and it's a nice day. Enjoy that morning, because it's a massive gift. Every day we know the sun will rise and we'll have a new day, so we get used to it. But it's always there. We can't put a price on it; we can't buy it; we can't sell it. These things? These things are beautiful.

Epilogue

Impossible Is a Dare is the story of our fight to see people set free
from slavery. Your 'impossible' might be the same; your 'impossible'
might be something different. Regardless of your dream, I hope
you've found thoughts, challenges and experiences in this book
that will prompt you to pursue that dream with passion, purpose
and persistence.

I wasn't ready to start Hope for Justice. If I'd known all that
it would demand, the cost to me, to my family, to others, I don't
know if I'd have done it. And that's why I'm so glad I started before
I was ready, before I knew what it meant. When I first had the
vision to hold a massive event to raise awareness of human trafficking, I didn't imagine it would be me doing it – I thought I wasn't
good enough, strong enough or mature enough. But the right
people believed in me and empowered me to achieve something
that has come further than I ever imagined.

If I'd waited until the time was perfect, until I was perfect,
Hope for Justice would never have happened. Perfectionism is the
enemy of a pioneering spirit: when you're trying to achieve
something new and outrageous, there's no way of really knowing
if you're ready; you just have to take a leap. We weren't ready; we
didn't know what would happen; we didn't know how to do it.

This is one reason why I'm so glad I've been surrounded by people with so much knowledge and expertise, to ensure we're professional and responsible in every area of our work. I'm not saying we hide our struggles or pretend to have skills we don't have. We don't try to be perfect – we try to be real; for us, being real involves not giving in to fear and doubt, and believing that some things are worth fighting for, tooth and nail.

At Hope for Justice we aim high and often punch above our weight. We try so hard not to become cynical and negative, because if you aim for the impossible, sometimes you actually achieve it. You have to make yourself vulnerable and risk disappointment in order to reach things no-one thinks you can. There are people living free from slavery because we reach for things others say are impossible. We say we want to end slavery – this isn't a strapline. People tell me it's impossible, that it will never happen, that the problem is too big. Your 'impossible' might feel the same. But if you don't even aim for it, then there's no chance you'll achieve it. You've been given your unique vision for a reason. Don't tell me it's impossible. Impossible is just a dare.